THE RESTORATION.

NOTICES OF THE PRESS.

"With Dr. Seiss we welcome the appearance of this book, and heartily recommend it to the Christian public as a production of a mature and candid mind, upon a subject exciting much attention at this time, and one that deserves the careful and candid consideration of every student of the Bible.

"The author is a strong thinker, an able writer, and a clear and logical reasoner; and we think no one with an unprejudiced mind, who will carefully weigh the arguments adduced, can fail to be convinced of the truth of the propositions they were intended to support." — *Western Recorder.*

"The writer has evidently made the thoughts his own, and honestly believes every word he has written. The style is elegant, perspicuous, and forcible, and the arguments in favor of his views are presented with fairness and candor."—*Presbyterian Index.*

"An attractive and interesting volume." —*Amer. Presbyterian.*

"Mr. Riley has been a popular and useful pastor, and he publishes this book because he feels that he has arrived at truth which the churches need. His views are presented clearly, vigorously, and in an excellent spirit. They are worthy of attention." *Christian Herald and Presbyterian Recorder.*

"It is an earnest, simple, and quite thorough presentation of what the author evidently in all honesty and conscientiousness believes is the truth on this subject. Besides the usual exposition of Scriptural passages bearing on this subject, he gives much historical and statistical information; and whether his views meet with general assent or not, any one may read his book with interest. Its tone, in regard to all who differ from the author, is Christian and good."— *Christian Instructor and Western United Presbyterian.*

NOTICES OF THE PRESS.

"The author has carefully studied the subject of the literal restoration of the Jews, and the premillenarian advent of Christ at his second coming, and has stated his views in a clear and sensible manner. We commend it to candid perusal." — *The Presbyterian.*

"For all who are favorable to the views it advocates, the work must possess more than usual interest. It is written in a lively, attractive, and forcible style, and furnishes evidence on every page, that the author is fully in earnest in the advocacy of his positions." — *German Reformed Messenger.*

"This little volume embodies the matter of a series of Sermons preached by the author to his congregation a year or two since, and covers not only the special subject of the approaching Restoration of the chosen people to their own ancient land, but also a general consideration of the intimately associated topic of the Premillennial Advent of our Lord. In the language of Dr. Seiss' Introduction, 'it is a work of a sober, mature, and candid mind, conscious of having something important to communicate. . . . . It ably deals with the great questions of the course of future Providence, and the consummation, for which our religion teaches us to hope. It makes no pretensions, but is full of important truth, fairly deduced, popularly presented, and suitably enforced. It is "meat in due season," from a faithful steward, and a workman who need not be ashamed.' — This eulogy, we think, is no more than just, and we would cordially recommend the volume to all who are seeking an insight into the solemn subject of which it treats." — *Western Episcopalian.*

"The author marshals the Scriptural argument for what are known as the Millenarian views, better than any American author we have read on the subject." — *Conn. Churchman.*

"The questions discussed in this work are highly important, and every one should feel deeply interested in their proper solution. Whilst the author, in the main, follows closely in the footsteps of others who have written upon the Millennium, he has succeeded in imparting new interest to the subject. Without indorsing all that the book contains, we regard it as a most interesting work, and cheerfully recommend it to our readers as one worthy of a candid and careful perusal." — *Presbyterian Witness.*

NOTICES OF THE PRESS.

"The volume before us presents the Premillennial view in a clear and forcible manner; and whether the reader will agree with this or not, he ought to consider carefully what is advanced, and not reject it until he can do so upon assured Scriptural grounds. We commend this work to our brethren in the ministry." — *Evangelical Repository.*

"These views Mr. Riley sets forth and advocates with plainness and moderation, but at the same time with earnestness, and with no little power. The doctrines of the second Adventists are evidently gaining ground in this country. They are advocated in the present volume with a general sobriety of language and statement that cannot fail to win for them a candid hearing." — *S. S. Times.*

"This volume is one of the latest additions to the popular literature on the subject of the Premillennial Advent of Christ. It is the work of one who has been for many years the honored pastor of an important church in Pennsylvania. The book is the presentation in a modified form of a series of Sermons preached within a few years to the congregation over which the author was settled. His endeavor seems to have been to present the whole subject in a simple Scriptural light, relying on no arguments but those which come from a fair interpretation of the inspired Words, and turning aside to scarce any objection which is not drawn from the same source." — *New York Evangelist.*

"I have read the book with great satisfaction, and have no hesitation in recommending it as a valuable contribution to the literature of the subject. It has elements of popular adaptation, united with strength of presentation, and a fairness and candor of tone which will render it acceptable to the general reader, and very useful to the cause." — *Extract of a Letter from Jos. A. Seiss, D.D*

"It does not seem possible to controvert the positions taken." *W. H. P.*

"A valuable contribution to the literature of the subject. The honest seeker after truth will find this book a valuable help to satisfy and settle his mind, and open to him the proper grandeur and joyousness of the redemption that is in Christ Jesus." — *Jos. A. Seiss, D.D.*

THE RESTORATION

AT

THE SECOND COMING OF CHRIST.

A SUMMARY OF MILLENARIAN DOCTRINES.

"WHOM THE HEAVENS MUST RECEIVE UNTIL THE TIMES OF RESTITUTION OF ALL THINGS."—ACTS 3:21.

BY

REV. HENRY A. RILEY,
Late Pastor of the First Presbyterian Church, Montrose, Pa.

WITH
AN INTRODUCTION,
BY REV. J. A. SEISS, D.D.,
PHILADELPHIA.

PHILADELPHIA:
J. B. LIPPINCOTT & CO.
1868.

PREFACE.

One of the subjects proposed for consideration, at the "Annual Week of Prayer," in January, 1863, had respect to the *Jews*. At that time the writer took occasion to remark that he believed that God had special and gracious purposes to accomplish, in reference to that remarkable people; that he fully anticipated their literal restoration to the land of their fathers; when they would be distinguished amid the nations of the earth and recognized as the Lord's "covenant people;" always remembered and cared for, during these centuries of dispersion, judicial blindness, and judgment. It was further remarked that as time would not then permit any more than this bare allusion to the subject, it would, perhaps, be made the theme of future discussion in the pulpit. Accordingly three discourses were prepared and delivered, on the present condition and future prospects of the Jewish people.

Having fulfilled this engagement, the writer's mind was deeply impressed with the importance—

the duty he may say—of presenting to his charge some of those great affiliated truths, so intimately associated with the subject discussed; to which he had been led, himself, to give attention, and in which he had become deeply interested. He accordingly delivered several discourses, purporting to give a sketch of the prominent doctrines of *Millenarianism;* hoping, without fully discussing the subject, to awaken an interest in the study of the prophecies, now in the process of fulfilment, or soon to be accomplished.

Recently the hand of the Lord was laid upon the writer. Prostrated by severe indisposition, during which for some days it was doubtful what might be the issue, his thoughts were much upon these great themes, which came to his remembrance with delightfully refreshing influence, as he thought he might be passing through "the dark valley." And it was at this time, with profound gratitude to God and with great comfort to his spirit, that he remembered that, before closing a pastorate of five-and-twenty years, he had been led to present to his people what he now feels, most fully, to be the truth, in reference to some subjects, which, in his earlier ministry, were not, he thinks, correctly apprehended, and hence not scripturally exhibited.

It moreover became with him, in his convalescence, a serious question whether he should not give to the public what had, during his illness, been to him the cause of much thankfulness and of much comfort, with the hope that some, thereby, might be induced more carefully to "search the Scriptures *whether these things were so.*"

With these impressions, although aware that the subject as presented is very imperfectly exhibited, he sends forth this little volume, it being the substance of the sermons given to his people, but somewhat modified in its arrangement. It is divided into chapters, with the omission of portions which were more especially appropriate to discourses publicly delivered, than to discussions of important subjects to be read and carefully pondered. Those who heard the discourses will find, on reading the volume, the addition of some topics of special interest.

And now, all that is requested, is a candid, careful and prayerful examination of the subject, notwithstanding any seeming difficulties it may at first present, and notwithstanding its antagonism to preconceived and long and fondly cherished views of a spiritual coming and reign of Christ, and of a *Millennium* of the Church without and *before* His glorious "*Epiphany.*"

If these things are not in accordance with the teachings of divine truth, they should be, without hesitation, rejected. But if they are, in verity, the revelations of the Holy Spirit, it is of the utmost importance that we should know it, and embrace them and yield to their practical influence.

It will not do to assume it as a settled fact that they are erroneous, because we have been taught so from our earliest childhood; for momentous personal interests may be involved, as there certainly are involved interests of incalculable importance to the Church and to the world. Therefore should every reader, and especially *every commissioned teacher of holy things*—every minister of Christ—make diligent inquiry; *Can we in these latter days meet our responsibilities without a careful investigation of this subject?*

"Blessed is he that *readeth*, and they that *hear* the words of *this* prophecy, and *keep* those things which are written therein; *for the time is at hand.*" (Rev. 1:3.)

H. A. R.

MONTROSE, PA., December, 1865.

INTRODUCTION.

THE history of this book is given in the Preface, and its scope, in the Table of Contents. Each reader will, of course, form his own opinion concerning it. But a word of introduction may not be out of place.

It is the work of a sober, mature, and candid mind, conscious of having something important to communicate. It treats of the purposes and promises of God, as they are revealed to us in the Scriptures. It is a book on unfulfilled prophecy; just that department in which books and sound instruction are most needed, in these days. It ably deals with the great questions of the course of future Providence, and the consummation for which our religion teaches us to hope. It makes no pretensions, but is full of important truth, fairly deduced, popularly presented, and suitably enforced. It is "meat in due season," from a faithful steward, and a workman who need not be ashamed. It deserves a respectful, unprejudiced and devout examination. The honest seeker after the truth, who has not found it on these topics, will find this book a valuable help to satisfy and settle his mind, and to open to him the proper grandeur and joyousness of the "Redemption that is in Christ Jesus." We welcome its appearance, and heartily commend it to the Christian public.

Popular and satisfactory books of this sort, are scarce in this country. We need more of them. People have not encouraged the publication of them as they should, nor given them the attention which the importance of the subject demands. They have not sufficiently cared to know what God has given for our learning, concerning what must shortly come to pass. It is to be hoped that this state of things will not continue. The stir and cry; "Behold, the Bridegroom cometh!" are becoming too intense to be any longer disregarded with safety. If there are any wise virgins, they have no time to lose, nor opportunities to waste. They have need to arise, trim their lamps, review their ground, adjust their views to God's literal Word, and look up, wait and watch. And it is time for all to awake out of sleep; the night is far spent, the day is at hand, the judgment is near. Any hour may bring us to the resurrection of the dead. This present generation is the one which is to witness the Lord's return. Then let people beware, post themselves thoroughly in what the Scriptures foretell, and be ready, as the Saviour has enjoined; for "He that shall come, will come, and will not tarry."

PHILADELPHIA, December, 1865.

CONTENTS.

CHAPTER V.

CHAPTER VI.

CHAPTER VII.

CHAPTER VIII.

CHAPTER IX.

CHAPTER X.

CHAPTER XI.

SUMMARY AND CONCLUSION.

THE RESTORATION.

CHAPTER I.

THE JEWS.

A CRISIS AT HAND—THE JEWS INVOLVED IN IT—A WIDELY SCATTERED AND AFFLICTED PEOPLE—YET EVER PRESERVING THEIR DISTINCT NATIONALITY—A DIVINE PROVIDENCE SECURING THE ACCOMPLISHMENT OF A DIVINE PURPOSE—JERUSALEM TRODDEN DOWN OF THE GENTILES—JUDEA A BARREN LAND—A PROBLEM FOR INFIDELITY TO SOLVE—THE LAND TO BE RESTORED TO ITS FORMER FERTILITY—AND WHEREFORE?

And they shall fall by the edge of the sword, and shall be led away captive into all nations: and Jerusalem shall be trodden down of the Gentiles, until the times of the Gentiles be fulfilled. Blindness in part is happened to Israel until the fulness of the Gentiles be come in.—LUKE 21:24; ROM. 11:25.

THE future of our world is big with startling incidents. Can any one read the Sacred record, and note the significant signs of the times, without the conviction, that there is a grand prophetic era approaching, involving the interests of the Church of the living God, the destinies of the nations of the earth, and the Kingdom of the Lord Jesus Christ? Never, perhaps, in the history of the race, have events seemed to be so rapidly hastening on a most momentous crisis as in these very days in which we live. And careful students of the prophecies reach the conclusion that these events, startling in their nature as they are, effecting, or threatening to effect signal revolutions amid the nations, are but the providential premonitions of the near advent of the grand scenes which are to close the present period, and which were foreseen and made known by Daniel, by Isaiah, by Jeremiah, by Ezekiel, and by other inspired seers of the former dispensation; by St. Paul, by St. John, and by Jesus, the divine Teacher himself.

Prophecy presents to us a picture of the future of most absorbing interest, whatever be the mode of interpretation adopted. But especially is it so with those who believe, that the predictions of the Word of God are to be literally and not spiritually understood; that is, that the predicted *Millennium* is not the expansion and universal diffusion of the Gospel, resulting in a season of unprecedented religious prosperity,—the consummation of the present evangelical dispensation, and to be brought about by the instrumentalities now employed and by the efforts now put forth by the Church—but a new dispensation, to be miraculously introduced at the personal advent of Christ, which is to be a new and glorious development of Almighty power and grace and justice; when the saints of all past ages shall return with the Son of man to the earth, and with their resurrected bodies shall live and reign with Him, who, personally, literally present, as Zion's glorious Prince, shall administer His blessed Kingdom of universal righteousness and peace.

Intimately associated with the commencement of this state of things—immediately preceding, accompanying, or directly following the advent of the Redeemer, will be a series of other wonderful events, changing entirely the aspect of the social, political, and moral condition of existing nations. Prominent amid the actors of these scenes will be the Jews, that remarkable nation, whose prophetic history of the future, in at least one of its particulars, is the special subject of our discussion. We refer to their *predicted literal restoration* to the land of their former sojourn—the land promised to their forefathers for a *perpetual* occupancy.

Agreeably to the declaration of Scripture, they were to fall by the edge of the sword, and to be led away captive, or reduced to a most dependent, oppressed condition, among the kingdoms of the earth. Jerusalem was to be trodden down of the Gentiles, *until* the time of the Gentiles should be fulfilled, and blindness in part was to happen to Israel, *until* the fulness of the Gentiles should come in; evidently implying that at the fulfilment of that time, redemption should be their blessed experience. That they are to look on Him whom their forefathers have pierced and mourn in bitterness of soul, is the assurance of the prophet. They are thus to be led to recognize in Jesus Christ, their long-expected Messiah, and, by that acknowledgment, to secure to themselves again the manifested favor of their Lord, under whose frowns they have spent many wearisome centuries of anxious but fruitless anticipation of the advent of their Deliverer.

This recognition of Jesus of Nazareth as their Messiah, and their consequent conversion to Christianity, it is supposed, by one class of interpreters, are to be brought about while they are in their present widespread dispersion, and by direct missionary efforts of the Church to evangelize them. It is to be done, it is thought, by the gradual diffusion of Gospel truth by instrumentalities now employed. It is by *all* expected that many of them will be brought to a saving knowledge of Christ Jesus in this way. Numbers are thus rejoicing in a discovered Saviour in our day, and many more may thus be blessed. These constitute, however, perhaps, what is termed by St. Paul, the "election of grace;" and of these the Apostle thus speaks in the eleventh chapter of the Epistle to the Romans, and in immediate connection, it should be noticed, with the declaration of their rejection as a nation: "Even so then at this present time also there is a remnant according to the *election of grace.*" . . . "What then? Israel" (that is as a nation) "hath not obtained that which he seeketh for;" (namely, their promised Messiah,) "but the *election*" (some of the people) "hath obtained it, and the *rest* were blinded;" and to be blinded, the Saviour himself declares, until some future period, called the "times and the fulness of the Gentiles." But not to anticipate a fuller discussion of this subject we may particularly note, as bearing directly on our theme, and needful to its proper understanding:

First.—*That the Hebrew people are literally a widely scattered nation, and have been a distinct people from the earliest period of their history to the present time, now upwards of three thousand years.*

This fact presents one of the most remarkable phenomena in the history of the world. The first prophecy relative to the Jewish nation, distinctly as such, was that to Abraham at Ur of the Chaldees, as he received the call to leave his country and his kindred, and to go to the land that should be shown unto him. "I will make of thee," saith Jehovah, "a great nation." (Gen. 12: 2.) A solitary traveller, crossing the Euphrates, not knowing whither he went, but obeying the Divine voice which called him from among idolaters to become the father of a new people and of a purer faith, he repaired to Canaan. His grandson Jacob, "a Syrian ready to perish," went down into Egypt with a few individuals, where his descendants, during several years of prosperity, and several centuries of cruel bondage, became a nation, great and mighty—signally distinct from their oppressors—until delivered by a special interposition of Heaven. We then trace them in their wilderness wanderings, and see them gaining possession of Canaan, with their peculiar social and political and religious institutions—a separate people. In their degeneracy they incurred the displeasure of their Ruler, and were given, successively, into the hands of Pagan enemies, whom they were compelled to serve. Still they were kept separate. When they called upon the Lord, He raised up special deliverers for them in the Judges, who brought them out of all their distresses, but without any internal change in their national constitution. They called for a regal government, and God gave them a king. Thus they continued for ages; a portion indeed rebellious against rightful authority, but the nation retaining its distinct existence amid the surrounding peoples. Reduced to captivity in Babylon, because of their sins, there, away from the sepulchres of their fathers, and deprived of their wonted religious privileges, they still remained a separate community, until their return to repossess and rebuild their desolated homes. Four or five centuries were to intervene between their return from Babylon, and the advent of the Messiah. They were called to pass through various and trying scenes. Their city was captured by Alexander of Macedon, who sought by flattering privileges to seduce them into compliance with Pagan practices. It subsequently fell under the tyranny of Antiochus Epiphanes, a Syrian prince, who razed to the ground its walls, and ttempted, by bitter persecutions, to force them into idolatry. He sacrificed swine, the especial abomination of the Jew, upon the holy altar, erected new altars for the obligatory worship of Olympian Jupiter, burnt the Hebrew Scriptures, prohibited circumcision, and made every act of opposition a capital crime, to be punished with extreme cruelty.

Under the Maccabees they recovered their independence, which they enjoyed for a brief period, when, sinking into comparative insignificance in the political world, they were conquered by the Romans. To them they became tributary, as a vanquished nation, while yet they continued rigidly to maintain their distinguishing peculiarities, remaining a separate people, socially and religiously, until the birth of Christ. Then, indeed, a great change was to be wrought in their condition. Jerusalem had been a special bond of union. There, except during the seventy years' captivity, and during the bitter persecutions of Antiochus, they could meet for their religious observances. And, as their cherished memories and their warmest affections clustered around that sacred spot, it seemed the more closely to unite the nation in sympathy and in interest.

But for their iniquity, now culminating in the rejection of their Messiah, their city was to be laid waste and trodden down of the Gentiles, for many generations, and they were to be scattered to every quarter, even the remotest portions, of the globe. And we follow them in their wanderings for eighteen centuries, until, in our day, we find them so widely scattered that there is scarcely a known country on earth where they are not to be found. And the remarkable fact of their absolute separation, as a peculiar people, remains as strongly marked as at any previous time. In their social habits, in their religious observances, in their very cast of countenance, in all of the peculiarities which in ages past distinguished them, they are still a distinct people, although brought directly in contact, politically and in business transactions, with those with whom they reside. Milman thus speaks of them: "Refusing still to mingle their blood with any other race of mankind, they dwell in their distinct families and communities, and still maintain the principles of national unity. Jews in the indelible features of the countenance, in mental character, in customs, usages and laws, in language and literature, above all in religion, in the recollections of the past and in the hopes of the future, with ready pliancy they accommodate themselves to every soil, every climate, every gradation of manners and civilization, and every form of government. With inflexible pertinacity they practice their ancient usages, very rarely form matrimonial connections out of their own communion, and observe the fasts and festivals of their church. Denizens everywhere, rarely citizens. Even in the countries in which they have been the longest and most firmly established, they appear, to a certain degree, strangers or sojourners. They dwell apart, although mingling with their neighbors in many of the affairs of life. For common purposes they adopt the language of the country they inhabit; but the Hebrew remains the national tongue in which their holy books are read and their religious services conducted."[1]

The number of existing Jews is supposed at least to equal that of the most prosperous days of their history. It has been variously estimated from five to fourteen millions; and these, although for ages scattered among the various nations of the earth, existing under every climate, in every region, and under every form of government, retain their identity as a people, resisting all the influences calculated to merge them in and make them one with the people among whom they live. They present one of the most wonderful and interesting of all phenomena in the history of man. In this one particular, they stand alone. No other people under heaven have remained distinct for any length of time, even with but a tithe of the influences which are around them to cause them to lose their identity.

A few ages since, swarms of the northern nations overran the more southern parts of Europe. Where are they now to be found? The Gauls went forth in great bodies to seek their fortunes in foreign parts. What traces or footsteps of them are remaining now anywhere? But we need not specify. The records of all past generations may be challenged to produce anything like this fact in the history of the Hebrew people. And the more especially wonderful is it because, we repeat, of the strong inducements they have had to merge

[1] Milman's History of the Jews.

themselves in the nations among whom they have lived, and where they still reside, and thus to lose their distinctive peculiarities. This separate, distinct position which they have occupied, has been to them the cause of almost incredible evils.

Read the curses for disobedience, as recounted in the 28th and subsequent chapters of Deuteronomy, and then note the literal infliction of them upon this devoted people, many of them continued to our own day: "The Lord shall scatter thee among all people, from one end of the earth even unto the other. . . . And among these nations shalt thou find no ease, neither shall the sole of thy foot have rest." Most literally verified has been the prediction. The history of this people is the history of severe persecutions, inflicted upon them by almost every nation among whom they have lived. And all this oppressive treatment have they received because of their rigid adherence to the faith, the usages, and the hopes of their fathers. This they have known and keenly felt. And they know as well that it is because of their fathers' sins that they are thus under the frown of heaven.

Recently, there stood up in the Henry Street Synagogue, New York,[1] a young preacher, who, with fervid eloquence, thus addressed his people: "My brethren, it was indeed a dark day in the history of our nation when we sinned against God. No step could have been more fatal; no folly more

[1] New York Observer. January 1, 1863.

disastrous; no act as pregnant with misery and suffering. God alone can tell how *swift*, how *just*, and how terrible has been the retribution. Long years of misery, anguish, and suffering have been ours. For ages have we been wanderers upon the face of the earth, a byword and a reproach among the nations with whom our lot was cast. The iron heel of persecution has trampled us in the dust. The finger of scorn has pointed us out as the vilest of the vile. Our homes have been desecrated, our cities pillaged, our synagogues defiled. The hell-hounds of bigotry and superstition have pursued us with unrelenting hate from place to place. The torture, the stake, and the scaffold have ever been before our eyes. The iron of bitter anguish has ever been entering our souls. Hated, scoffed, despised, accounted as the veriest scum of the earth, incarcerated in filthy dungeons, starved, tortured, murdered, slain, until the pent-up agony of our souls, bursting from its care-worn fetters, almost compelled us to exclaim, like Cain of old, 'My punishment is greater than I can bear!'"

Thus spake the preacher with the emotions of deep conviction. Strong as this language is, it fails to picture fully the reality of the sufferings of this remarkable people. The strongest of earthly inducements have been held out to them to lead to an abandonment of their peculiarities and their exclusiveness. But all in vain. With wonderful tenacity they have maintained their separate existence.

This continuance of the Jews as a distinct community, amid their wide dispersion among the nations of the earth, is a most remarkable phenomenon, of which we may not lose sight, and the more especially because of the predicted future of their history.

A noteworthy prophecy, uttered 1400 years before the Christian era, foretold this state of things. Said Balaam, as he looked down upon the camp of Israel when he was bidden of Balak to curse: "How shall I curse whom God hath not cursed, or how shall I defy whom the Lord hath not defied? For from the top of the rock I see him, and from the hills I behold him. Lo! the people shall dwell *alone, and shall not be reckoned among the nations.*" (Num. 23:8, 9.) How literally has this prediction, uttered three thousand years ago, been verified! How literally has it its fulfilment in our own day!

Now, upon what principle is it to be accounted for, that, contrary to all observation and experience in every other case, this people should be preserved in its absolute unity, in its distinct and separate existence, for so many centuries, and in the face of so many powerful influences calculated to destroy it? Infidelity has attempted a solution; but it fails to meet the question. There it stands, a fact, without a parallel, to provoke inquiry; a problem, without explanation by worldly wisdom. It surely is not by mere chance that it is so. It cannot be ascribed to accident. In nothing can we find an answer *but in the direct, imme-*

diate agency of God—a divine providence securing the accomplishment of a divine purpose. The hand of God is as signally manifested in this thing, as in any miracle of former days. And is this anything less than a miracle, continued in its operation from generation to generation, an abiding testimony to the truthfulness of the prophetic Scriptures, a palpable and lasting rebuke to skepticism? But why is this people thus preserved by a direct Divine providence? An answer to this inquiry we may find before we close our discussion.

A SECOND fact demanding serious consideration is, *that Jerusalem is to be trodden down of the Gentiles during this dispersion of the Jews.* It was so predicted by ancient prophets, and so foretold by the Saviour himself. "And, accordingly, Jerusalem hath never since been in the possession of this people; but constantly has it been in subjection to some other nation. First to the Romans, afterwards to the Saracens, then to the Franks, subsequently to the Mamelukes, and now to the Turks," whose crescent has taken the place of the ensign of the tribe of Judah. It has been literally trodden down of the Gentiles for the last eighteen centuries.

The words and feelings of Jeremiah are the appropriate expression of the sorrowing Christian heart in our day; as scoffing ones "pass by and clap their hands at her; they hiss and wag their heads at the daughter of Jerusalem, saying, 'Is this the city that men call the perfection of beauty, the joy of the whole earth?'"

Dr. Fisk, who, a few years since, visited Jerusalem, remarks: "Many a time has the question been asked me, What is the precise impression that Jerusalem made and left upon your mind? The most carefully graphic and elaborate answer that I feel capable of offering, would fall far short of that which is given by Jeremiah in the book of Lamentations, in every sentence of which one seems to trace the trickling of a tear, the breathing of a deep-drawn sigh—the tear and the sigh hopeless and heartless—of Jerusalem, for the glory that *is departed.*" Doubtless the prophet depicted Jerusalem as he saw her when the avenging hand of Jehovah first laid her honor in the dust. But he did more than that. With a prophet's vision he foresaw the utter desolation which impended, in times which should be big with the most disastrous events towards her, when Jerusalem should become "heaps," and be finally, as she is now, trodden down of the Gentiles. And all that Jeremiah foretold as a prophet, and everything he recorded as an historian, is at any moment to be traced in the present aspect of the Holy City and her miserable population. Exaggeration is almost impossible upon the condition of the Jews at the present day. And what is said of Jerusalem, is true of the whole land of Palestine. By Moses it was described as "a good land, a land of brooks of water, of fountains and depths that spring out of valleys and hills; a land of wheat, and barley, and vines, and fig-trees, and pomegranates; a land of oil, olives and honey; a land wherein thou shalt eat bread without scarceness. Thou shalt not lack anything in it." (Deut. 8 : 7–9.) By the Lord himself it was called "the glory of all lands." But this land, once most remarkable for its fertility, is now but little more than a barren waste; and as the traveller looks over the scene of sterility, he inquires, Can these stony hills, these deserted valleys, be indeed the land of promise, the land once flowing with milk and honey?" "Above all other countries in the world, it is now a land of ruins."[1] Evidences of former fertility are said to abound on every hand, while they appear but in noted contrast to its present wretched condition. "The more," writes Paxton, "I see of Palestine, the more I am persuaded that it was once one of the finest countries in the world." Now poverty, wretchedness and barrenness are its general characteristics. This state of Jerusalem and this condition of the land, once the luxurious residence of a favored nation, are but the literal fulfilment of prophetic declarations.

One who but recently looked upon these very scenes of desolation writes: "The numerous prophecies concerning Canaan have been so literally fulfilled that they may be used as actual history. It is now under the curse of God, and its general barrenness is in full accordance with prophetic denunciation." "Your land," said Jehovah to his people, when warning them against disobe-

[1] Stanley.

dience, "Your land shall be desolate and your cities waste." (Lev. 26:33.) Jeremiah speaks as one looking upon a scene of sadness actually spread out before him, so vividly before his eye was Canaan's coming desolation depicted. "They have destroyed my vineyard. They have trodden my portion under foot. They have made my pleasant portion a desolate wilderness. They have made it desolate. The whole land is made desolate." (12:10, 11.)

Thus we have before our minds, as scenes actually existing in our day, the wide dispersion of the Jewish people, and their separation from the land of their fathers; their present wanderings in every quarter of the globe; their bitter persecutions and severe sufferings, and injurious, ignominious treatment, for successive centuries; the destruction of their holy city, and its continuing desecration by Gentile feet and by Gentile usages; and the utter desolation of the land where their ancestors dwelt as in the heritage of the Lord—then a land of fertility and plenty. And all this in exact fulfilment of prophecy.

The question now arises, is this condition of things always to exist? Are these millions of Jews—once the honored, favored people of God—always to remain in their dispersion, retaining still their peculiarities and their identity and oneness as a people? Or are they yet to become merged and lost in the various nations among whom they are so widely scattered? Are they to lay aside their distinctive character, and then to be brought to the knowledge of Christ and His salvation, and become one with the Gentile Church, by the gradual diffusion of the Gospel? If such is to be their condition, after eighteen centuries of a national separation from the different governments under which they have lived, and a preservation of their oneness as a people, without a parallel in the annals of the world—a preservation most clearly bespeaking the hand of an overruling Providence—then truly does their continued separate existence become a mystery; a mystery, indeed, admitting of no solution! Why, on this supposition, have they been thus preserved? Why so miraculously watched over and cared for?

But are they, in very deed, to pass thus silently from our view? Are they, in all their peculiarities, gradually to melt away and disappear like the morning hoarfrost, leaving no trace behind them? Are they to become thus quietly extinct? And is their holy city, the place of their fathers' solemnities, a spot made most sacred by the thousand hallowed memories which cluster around its sacred temple, its palaces, its altars, and its walls, always to be trodden down by Gentile feet, and to be desecrated by the godless mosque of Omar? And is that once fair land—bequeathed to the chosen people as an inheritance, a *perpetual* inheritance, a land of luxuriance under the fostering smiles of the Lord Jehovah—ever to remain the seared and desolate region which now it is, and which it has been for generations past?

Hear what Isaiah says, giving utterance to feelings which are as much the experience and the cry of the Jewish people in *our* day as they were of any generation past: "Be not wroth very sore, O Lord! neither remember iniquity forever; behold, see! we beseech Thee: we are all Thy people. Thy holy cities are a wilderness, Zion is a wilderness, Jerusalem a desolation. Our holy and beautiful house, where our fathers praised Thee, is burned up with fire; and all our pleasant things are laid waste. Wilt Thou refrain Thyself from these things, O Lord? Wilt Thou hold Thy peace, and afflict us very sore?" (Is. 64: 9–12.) Such is Jerusalem, as trodden down of the Gentiles. Note, now, the subsequent declaration—a fitting response to this bitter cry: "Be ye glad and rejoice forever in that which I create: for behold! I create Jerusalem a rejoicing, and her people a joy. And I will rejoice in Jerusalem and joy in my people; and the voice of weeping shall be heard no more in her, nor the voice of crying." "And they shall build houses and inhabit them, and they shall plant vineyards and eat the fruit of them." (Is. 65 : 18, 19, 21.) A prediction far from being met, in its prophetic import, by the rebuilding of the city after the captivity at Babylon, for, as the context shows, it looked forward to the more glorious times of the second advent of the Messiah. And so Zechariah, speaking of the same anticipated time, says: "It shall be in that day that living waters shall go out from Jerusalem, . . . and the Lord shall be King over *all* the earth. In that day shall there be one Lord. All the land shall be turned as a plain, from Geba to Rimmon, south of Jerusalem, and it shall be lifted up and inhabited in her place, from Benjamin's gate unto the place of the first gate, and men shall dwell in it, and there shall be no more utter destruction, but Jerusalem shall be safely inhabited." (14: 8–11.) Of this passage, Dr. Scott says: "Jerusalem, which has long been trodden down of the Gentiles, will be raised up from that debased condition, and rebuilded to the whole of her former extent, and inhabited throughout. It shall no more be devoted to utter destruction under the awful curse of God, but it will become a serene and peaceful habitation."

"Behold," says Jeremiah, "the days come that the city shall be built to the Lord. . . It shall not be plucked up nor thrown down any more." (31: 38, 40.) "I will call," writes Ezekiel, "for the corn and will increase it, and I will multiply the fruit of the tree and the increase of the field." . . . . . . "And they shall say, this land which was desolate is become like the garden of Eden." (36 : 29, 30, 35.) "The Lord shall comfort Zion: He will comfort all her waste places. He will make her wilderness like Eden and her desert like the garden of the Lord." (Is. 51 : 3.)

And never yet have the glowing words of Isaiah, as recorded in the sixtieth chapter of his prophecy, met with anything like their fulfilment. They anticipate the glorious results of Christ's mediatorial work to be witnessed here on earth; and in the midst of his enrapturing state ments, he declares: "And the sons of strangers shall build up thy walls, and their kings shall minister unto thee. For in my wrath I smote thee, but in my favor have I had mercy on thee. Therefore thy gates shall be open continually; they shall not be shut day nor night." (60: 10, 11.) Thus have we the assurance that Jerusalem, long forsaken, desolate, and trodden down, shall be restored to more than her former grandeur, and the land, now laid waste and blighted, shall regain its former fruitfulness. But wherefore these changes? Why—for what purpose—shall now debased Jerusalem be rebuilt? and for what purpose, and by whom, the desolate land be made once more to bloom and blossom as the rose?

These predictions, it should be remembered, were given to the Jewish people. Were these prophetic declarations of the rebuilding of their loved and honored city, of its restoration to grandeur and safety, and becoming a place of habitation, and of the returning luxuriance and fertility of the land, meant to mock their misery and to add to their humiliation in their wide dispersion—as most grievously they would if they were no more themselves to look upon the renovated glory of the one, and to enjoy the fruitfulness of the other?

In answer to the question, "Wherefore these predicted changes?" we remark that it is all in anticipation of the re-occupancy of Jerusalem, and the land promised to Abraham and his seed, by the still outcast, wandering children of Israel, who are, if we read the prophetic record correctly, to be literally restored to the inheritance of their fathers, to worship again at Jerusalem, and to possess the land which is theirs by covenant engagement. If the prophecies in reference to the desolation of Palestine, the destruction of Jerusalem and its defilement by Gentile feet, and the wide dispersion of the Jewish people, their multiplied sorrows, and hardships, and persecutions, and their remaining a distinct, separate people in the very midst of their persecuting foes, who have sought to amalgamate them with the people and to induce them to cast aside their offensive peculiarities—if these prophecies have, in a most remarkable manner, met their exact literal fulfilment, by what process of reasoning, or by what law of interpretation, can we reach the conclusion that what of prophecy remains unfulfilled, touching the restoration of the Jews, is not to be as literally verified? If the former have been realized, will not the latter? And if the first have had a literal fulfilment, must not the second have the same? Can we look abroad over the dispersed Hebrew people, and be struck with the truthfulness of God as manifested in the precise verification of the words of the inspired prophets, and of Jesus himself—and then read the predictions, in reference to the same people, yet to be fulfilled, and say that our principles of interpretation are to be entirely changed, so that what appears to be a declaration literally to be accomplished, must have a spiritual import? Are we thus to read the sacred record? And yet there are those who believe that all that is said in reference to the return of the Jews, and their restoration to their own land, and the recovery of the ten lost tribes, with their reunion and re-establishment with the two tribes, as one nation, in Palestine, in more than the pristine glory of the Theocracy, is a mere *allegorical* description of their conversion and absorption into the Church while remaining in the lands of their dispersion; and this to be in connection with the ingathering of the Gentile nations into the fold of the Redeemer; all of which is to be accomplished by the gradual spread of evangelical truth, and by the means and efforts now put forth by the Church for this end! It may be that the word of God, correctly understood, will lead to a different conclusion. Our present discussion touches one definite point bearing on this general subject, namely, the literal return or restoration of the Hebrew people to the land of Palestine—an event most intimately connected with, and being, indeed, itself one of a series of manifestations of divine power and glory, which, it is thought, are to mark the closing of the present dispensation, and which will be the theme of subsequent inquiry.

CHAPTER II.

THE JEWS, CONTINUED.

RESTORATION OF THE JEWS—WHO ARE THE JEWS?—JUDAH AND ISRAEL—THE LOST TEN TRIBES—JEWS CHERISH THE EXPECTATION OF A LITERAL RESTORATION—WAILING-PLACE AT JERUSALEM— THEIR INIQUITY THE ACKNOWLEDGED CAUSE OF THEIR AFFLICTIONS —CONSTANT READINESS TO DEPART.

I say, then, hath God cast away his people? God forbid. God hath not cast away his people whom he foreknew.—ROMANS, 11 : 1, 2.

THOSE here spoken of and designated the people of God, "*his people*," are the Jews, and with peculiar propriety and significancy are they thus styled, inasmuch as they were constituted a peculiar, separate people, by Divine appointment, and for many generations watched over and directly governed by Jehovah, as their immediate Head and Ruler, as they were made the recipients of manifold favors—the depository, indeed, of the blessings of the true religion, and a people with whom a covenant had been made of abiding mercy: "Who are Israelites; to whom pertaineth the adoption, and the glory, and the covenants, and the giving of the law, and the service of God, and the promises." Rom. 9 : 4.

"The world having been visited with the signal judgments of heaven, because of man's increasing iniquity, Noah became the second progenitor of the race; and we find, in the history immediately following the deluge, mention made of three distinct lines of descent—one from each of the patriarch's sons, Japheth, Ham, and Shem. After the dispersion of the people from Babel, one hundred years subsequent to the deluge, tne descendants of Shem are again introduced, and carried down to the family of Terah. Ham and Japheth are lost sight of in the history for a season, and Shem is taken. All the other descendants of Shem are then lost sight of, and Terah is taken; and all the sons of Terah are lost sight of, and Abraham is taken; and on him and his posterity the whole attention of the reader of the sacred record is concentrated."[1]

Receiving a divine call, Abraham repaired to Canaan, and became the father of that remarkable nation, whose history had been fraught with such peculiar interest, and whose destiny had been most intimately and manifestly interwoven with all the purposes of infinite wisdom, up to the time the Apostle penned his letter to the Romans. They had become an exceedingly degenerate people, and for their sins they had been severely punished; and now, as a nation, for their rejection of their Messiah, they were shut out from the special manifestation of the Divine favor, and the blessings of salvation were bestowed upon the Gentiles. With Abraham and his immediate descendants the

[1] McNeile.

Lord had entered into a gracious covenant, promising not only a numerous posterity, but rich, distinguishing mercies, of which they were never to be dispossessed. As these covenanted promises, in the full extent of the assurance, had not been realized to them, so to the future were they to look for the verification of all that God had spoken. In the 11th chapter of his Epistle to the Romans, St. Paul states that judicial blindness was, for a season, to remain on this nation, because of their unbelief, during which they were to be under the manifested displeasure of their offended Ruler; a people scattered amid the nations of the earth, frowned upon and outcast. The purposed period, however, being accomplished—the fulness of the Gentiles having come in—the vail is to be taken from off their minds, and the blessings of the covenant, made with their ancestors, and which could not be annulled "(for the gifts and calling of God are without repentance)," are to be theirs, in rich and full experience. As the past history of the Jews has been most intimately associated with the hopes of an apostate race, so is all that is cheering and hopeful and blessed in the future as intimately connected with God's dealings with them. They are to bear a most important part in those startling scenes which are to close the present dispensation, and to usher in that period when the prophecies of the second advent of the Son of God, previous to the millennium, of the resurrection of the pious dead, of the destruction of the Antichristian nations, and the reign of Christ on earth, are to be literally verified. At that time they are to discover their error and sin in rejecting the Messiah, and to turn to him whom they have pierced, with bitter lamentation and confession, and yet with exultant hearts, at finding him of whom Moses and the Prophets did speak. Preceding this change, they are to be gathered from their wide dispersion among the nations, and restored to the actual possession of Palestine, in fulfilment of the covenant engagement made with Abraham, and in accomplishment of innumerable predictions of the prophets. This is the special subject of our discussion.

As preliminary to a consideration of the proof of it, attention has been directed to a few facts, one of which was the actual dispersion of the Jewish people among the nations of the earth, a fact arresting the notice of the most heedless observer; for wherever the explorer goes, amid whatever people he sojourns, in every clime, under every government, there, in greater or less numbers, are to be found representatives of the Hebrew race. This is but the literal fulfilment of prophecies, uttered centuries before there was the slightest reason, from their condition, to anticipate such an event. But what renders it a fact of special interest, and of most wonderful significancy, is, as we have noticed, the maintenance of their absolute individuality among and separation from the various peoples amid whom they live in their dispersion. This fact has been sufficiently illustrated. It is a constantly perpetuated miracle, showing a Divine agency, and a signal providential care over them. We have also seen how literally the predictions in reference to Jerusalem and the once luxuriant land have been fulfilled; the former, their Holy City, being wrested from their hands and trodden down of the Gentiles; and the latter having become a barren waste, blighted, seared, desolate, under the frowning providence of God. The city, however, is to be rebuilt, and restored to its former glory; and the land is again to be blessed with its former fertility. So the voice of prophecy distinctly declares; and the emphatic question is suggested, *For what purpose has the providence of God been thus exercised?* The only satisfactory solution may be found, perhaps, in the prediction touching the return of this people to their city and the land of their fathers, and their actual possession and enjoyment of it, agreeably to the covenant made with Abraham of old. Many are the prophecies bearing upon this event, and nothing but a fulfilment of them, as literal as that in reference to their dispersion and their preservation, and the destruction of their city and land, can solve the question.

But who are we to understand by the Jews? Who are they who are to be restored?

Jacob, after having wrestled successfully with the angel-Jehovah at Penuel,[1] was called *Israel*, a

[1] Gen. 32:24; Hos. 12:4.

name subsequently given to his posterity, embracing the twelve tribes who were known as *Israelites.* And thus it continued until the revolt of ten of the tribes, at the instigation of Jeroboam; when these, the rebel portion of the people, established an independent government, with their seat at Samaria, and were known as the *Kingdom of Israel;* and the remaining loyal tribes of Benjamin and Judah, with their seat at Jerusalem, were known as the *Kingdom of Judah.* Thus they continued for three centuries; the two kingdoms being governed by independent rulers.

For their sins, both were carried into captivity; first, the kingdom of Israel to Assyria, and then that of Judah to Babylon. At the expiration of the predicted seventy years' captivity of Judah, permission was given them to return, rebuild their desolate city, and repossess the land. But it is a noticeable fact, that but very few of the ten tribes, or the kingdom of Israel, were united with them in this enterprise.

As a body they were not restored, and so it was foretold. It was declared that they should be outcast, totally cut off from all visible interposition in their behalf, differing thus from the predicted dealings of God with Judah. They have passed entirely from view; and are known as the *lost* tribes.

Having totally revolted from God to the worship of golden calves, and having been guilty of excessive abominations, they were suffered to remain in the land of their captivity. It was a matter of special importance that *Judah* should remain in its distinct and separate condition, as a tribe and as families, until the coming of the Messiah, as He was to be of the tribe of Judah and of the family of David. The kingdom or commonwealth of Israel being destroyed, or utterly broken up, and the tribes constituting it being lost sight of, and those who returned to Palestine being mainly merged in the tribes of Judah and Benjamin, all were known as *Jews.* And in the New Testament, the name of the whole nation in its earlier ages, from Jacob to Rehoboam, is restored, and used generally to designate the Hebrew people. They were all Israelites. Paul calls himself an Israelite, in the same sentence in which he specifies the tribe of *Benjamin* as his paternal tribe. "I also am an Israelite, of the seed of Abraham, of the tribe of Benjamin." (Rom. 11:1.)

Those whose remarkable separation from the nations of the earth among whom they are scattered, who, in so wonderful a manner, are kept distinct, with the comparatively few of Israel who have become amalgamated with them, constitute the kingdom of Judah. Of these it was predicted that they should never lose the distinguishing badge of their identity as a separate people—the worshippers of the God of Abraham. Whereas, the ten tribes are lost to the eye of man, and were so several centuries before the advent of Christ; and by some it is maintained they are never to be found. Diligent search has been made for them, and some ingenious conjectures hazarded; but the search has been in vain, and the conjectures are without confirmation. Their present condition, as withdrawn from the manifested, recognized scene of God's providence, is the fulfilment of prophecies respecting them. But, although man cannot find them so as to identify them, the eye of the Omniscient is upon them, and from their seclusion they are to come forth to the glorious vindication of Jehovah's veracity; for both Israel and Judah are embraced in the coming restoration. Thus we find it written by Isaiah, in the glowing prophecies contained in the eleventh chapter, which has reference to the millennial times: "It shall come to pass *in that day*, that the Lord shall set his hand again, the *second time*, to recover the remnant of his people which shall be left from Assyria, and from Egypt, and from Pathros, and from Cush, and from Elam, and from Shinar, and from Hamath, and from the isles of the sea; and he shall set up an ensign for the nations, and shall assemble the outcasts of *Israel*, and gather together the dispersed of *Judah*,"—that is, the whole Jewish nation,—"from the four corners of the earth. The envy also of Ephraim shall depart, and the adversaries of Judah shall be cut off: Ephraim shall not envy Judah, and Judah shall not vex Ephraim. . . . . And there shall be a highway for the remnant of his people, which shall be left, from Assyria; like as it was to Israel in the day that he came up out of the land of Egypt." (Isaiah 11:11–16.) This surely has not yet met with its fulfilment.

In Jeremiah 31:15, it is said: "A voice was

heard in Ramah, lamentation and bitter weeping; Rachel, weeping for her children, refused to be comforted for her children, because they were not." Who were these children of Rachel, whose loss she lamented so bitterly? They were the ten tribes, or the kingdom of Israel, who, with Judah, were to be restored to their former possessions. To them the prophecy mainly refers, as appears from the repeated allusions to Ephraim, the head of these tribes; as also from the mention made of the mountains of *Samaria*, the metropolis of the kingdom, and of the watchmen upon Mount *Ephraim*, who are represented as calling upon the people to go up to Mount Zion for worship. Both kingdoms, the Jews, and Ephraim, or the ten tribes, are represented as already in possession of their own land, with all their former divisions healed. These ten tribes were those for whom Rachel thus bitterly wept. Rachel was the wife of Jacob, and the mother of Joseph and Benjamin. And Ephraim was the youngest son of Joseph. From him descended a very large proportion of the kingdom of Israel. These had been carried into captivity a century or more before this prophecy was uttered. The sepulchre of Rachel was between Ramah and Bethlehem. By a bold figure, she is represented as rising from the grave, and as looking round, and, seeing none of her offspring, is inconsolable in her sorrow, supposing them all utterly extirpated. But were they so? And were they never again to possess their former homes?

Note how her lamentations are met, and with what words the Lord is pleased to comfort her: "Thus saith the Lord: Refrain thy voice from weeping and thine eyes from tears; for thy works shall be rewarded, saith the Lord. *And they shall come again* from the land of the enemy, and there is hope in thine end, saith the Lord, *that thy children shall come again to their own border.*" (31:16,17.) Has this promise yet been verified? Surely, if the word of Jehovah be worthy of confidence, then a future restoration of these lost ten tribes is certain.

Turn now to Ezekiel, 37: 15: "The word of the Lord came unto me, saying, Moreover, thou son of man, take thou one stick and write upon it, *for Judah* and for the children of *Israel* his companions; then take another stick and write upon it, *for Joseph*, the *stick of Ephraim* and for all the house of Israel his companions; and join them one to another into *one* stick. And when the children of thy people shall speak unto thee, saying, 'Wilt thou not show us what thou meanest by these?' Say unto them, Thus saith the Lord God: . . . . Behold! I will take the children of Israel from among the heathen whither they be gone, and will gather them on every side, and *bring them into their own land;* and I will make them *one* nation in the land upon the mountains of Israel, and *one king* shall be *king to them all: and they shall be no more two nations, neither shall they be divided into two kingdoms any more at all.* Neither shall they defile themselves any more with their idols, nor with their detestable things, nor with any of their transgressions; . . . they shall be my people, and I will be their God. And *David my servant* shall be king over them, and they all shall have one shepherd, they shall also walk in my judgments and observe my statutes and do them. *And they shall dwell in the land that I have given unto Jacob my servant, wherein your fathers have dwelt; and they shall dwell therein, even they and their children and their children's children forever.* And my servant David shall be their prince *forever*." Does not this prediction most evidently look forward to the future for its fulfilment? Has anything in the past history of the Jews even approximated to an accomplishment of it? The two kingdoms of Judah and Israel have never been united, as is here foretold by the significant joining together of the two sticks. Israel as a people did not return from its captivity with Judah when the latter returned to Jerusalem from Babylon. It remains still, as the *lost* ten tribes, to be gathered home to Jerusalem, by the promise of God, when with Judah it shall constitute one nation, again blessed of heaven. And there, as one nation, they are to be governed *by one king*, and that king shall be David. We need scarcely remark that Christ is most obviously meant by this title, as a descendant of David. Moreover, it is a fact beyond dispute, even on the supposition that on their release from Babylon they became one kingdom, that they have never yet been governed as one nation, by any king to whom the name of

David could be given. "On their return from Babylon, no descendant of David, nor any line of kings of the family of David, ruled over the nation, but a series of governors, of whom the most remarkable are known to have been of other families. The Maccabees, who commenced their career of patriotic and religious heroism during the persecution of Antiochus Epiphanes, about one hundred and sixty years before the Christian era, and under whose services the kingdom enjoyed a brief period of independence, were Levites, concerning whose tribe neither Moses nor any other prophet speaks anything of royalty."[1]

They are, moreover, to dwell in their own land, and there to be governed by David, or Christ, *forever*. They are also to be purified from all their sins, and to be a holy people unto the Lord. Need we undertake to show that these predictions must be met by the *future* condition of the Jewish nation, if ever met? Note, again, the particulars of the prediction. The people are to be scattered among the nations of the earth; Judah and Israel are to be gathered from their dispersion; they are to be united as one people; to constitute one kingdom, never again to be divided into two kingdoms; they are to be brought to their *own land*, the land of their fathers, a land given to them by covenant engagement; there are they to dwell *forever;* they are to be separated from their transgressions, and made a holy people; David, or

[1] McNeile.

Christ, a lineal descendant of David, and often called by this name, is to reign over them, and his reign is to be *forever;* and the sanctuary of God is to be in the midst of them *forevermore.* The simple question is, Is there anything in the past history of the Jews to answer to these statements? If so, where is it to be found? Their return from Babylonish captivity does not meet it, as already stated; nor will this and similar predictions admit of a satisfactory spiritual interpretation; an interpretation which makes the *land* to mean the Church, the restoration to mean the conversion of the Jews to Christianity; the two kingdoms to mean Jews and Gentiles in one church; the one king to mean Jesus Christ, of the lineage and house of David, exercising spiritual dominion over all believers.

The prophecy was addressed to the *Hebrew people,* and obviously has exclusive reference to them; and as the prediction touching their wide dispersion, their separate existence amid the nations of the earth, the desolations of their land, the defilement of their holy city by Gentile feet and by Gentile usages, have all been fulfilled to the very letter, and as we have reason to believe from prophecy that Jerusalem is to be restored, and the land again blessed with even more than its former fruitfulness, shall we hesitate to say that these predictions, just as plain and positive as the others, are not to have as literal a fulfilment? The predictions are continuous, have respect to precisely the same people, specified by name.

Shall, then, all that is past be literal, and all that is future be figurative and spiritual? But what say other prophecies? Look for a moment at the declaration of Moses (Deut. 27 and 28 chh.), when at the command of God he set before the divided tribes, on Gerizim and Ebal, the blessings for obedience and the curses for disobedience. Read the list of these fearful curses. Then behold the spectacle the providence of God at this moment actually presents, and see how literally they are in our day, as they have been for generations past, in process of actual fulfilment. Their wide dispersion among the nations was a part of the threatening.

Hear, now, the words of Jehovah, as uttered upon that memorable occasion, three thousand years since, and say whether or not the declaration has yet been verified. "And it shall come to pass when all these things are come upon thee, the blessing and the curse which I have set before thee, and thou shalt call them to mind among all the *nations whither the Lord thy God hath driven thee;* and shalt return unto the Lord thy God, and shalt obey his voice, thou, and thy children, with all thine heart and with all thy soul; that then the Lord will turn thy captivity, and will have compassion upon thee, and *will return* and *gather thee from all the nations* whither the Lord thy God hath scattered thee. If any of thine be driven out unto *the utmost parts* of heaven, from thence will the Lord thy God *gather thee*, and from thence will he fetch thee. And the *Lord thy God will bring thee into the land which thy fathers prepared*, and thou shalt possess it." (Deut. 30.) Has this assurance yet been verified to this people? If so, we again inquire, and with emphasis, when, and where? From the *uttermost parts of heaven*, and from all the *nations of the earth*, they have never been gathered since their first dispersion. And is the prophecy that of a figurative or spiritual restoration and gathering? Is the predicted wide dispersion *literally* fulfilled? we once more inquire; and is not the *restoration* to be the same? Can we possibly understand it otherwise?

Read, now, in Isaiah 43: 5, 6. "Fear not, for I am with thee: I will bring thy seed from the east, and gather thee from the west. I will say to the *north*, give up; and to the *south*, keep not back: bring my sons from far, and my daughters *from the ends of the earth*." Here is the gracious assurance that this people, once highly favored, now under the Divine displeasure, shall be collected "from the *north*, and from the *south*, and from the *east*, and from the *west*, *even from the ends of the earth;*" and the context shows, that it is that they may again inherit their fathers' land. When returning from Babylon, they only came from the *north*. From the south, the east, and the west, they were not gathered. Of similar import is the declaration of Amos 9: 9, 14, 15: "I will not utterly destroy the house of Jacob, saith the Lord. For, lo, I will command, and I will *sift the house of Israel among all nations*, .. and I will bring again the captivity of my people Israel, and they shall build

6

the waste cities, and inhabit them; and they shall plant vineyards, and drink the wine thereof; they shall also make gardens and eat the fruit of them. And I will plant them upon their land, and they shall no more be pulled up out of their land which I have given them, saith the Lord thy God." And Jeremiah is equally explicit: "Behold, I will gather them out of all countries whither I have driven them in mine anger and in my fury, and I will bring them again unto this place, and I will cause them to dwell safely, and they shall be my people, and I will be their God, and I will give them one heart and one way, that they may fear me *forever;* and I will make an *everlasting* covenant with them, that I will not turn away from them to do them good. Yea, I will rejoice over them to do them good, and I will plant them in this land *assuredly* with my whole heart and with my whole soul." (32 : 37–41.) "And I will cause the captivity of Judah and the captivity of Israel to return, and will build them, as at the first. There shall be heard in this place, which ye say shall be desolate, without man and without beast, even in the cities of Judah and in the streets of Jerusalem, that are desolate, the voice of joy and the voice of gladness." (33: 7, 10.) Ezekiel writes: "Thus saith the Lord God: I will even gather you from the people and assemble you out of the countries where you have been scattered, and I will give you the land of Israel." (11 : 17.)

Upon the rich treasury of truth, upon this interesting theme, we will make but one more draft.

It is the testimony of one whose prophecy was uttered *after* the return from Babylon, and must consequently refer to the then future restoration. Zechariah prophesied several years after the captivity. He presents us with some of the most striking predictions of the Jewish people. Read as a specimen: "Thus saith the Lord; I am returned unto Zion, and will dwell in the midst of Jerusalem, and Jerusalem shall be called a city of truth; and the mountain of the Lord of hosts, the holy mountain. Thus saith the Lord of hosts; There shall yet old men and old women dwell in the streets of Jerusalem, and every man with his staff in his hand for very age. And the streets of the city shall be full of girls and boys playing in the streets thereof." (8 : 3–5.) A glowing picture of prosperity, peace, and enjoyment. But was not the prophet describing scenes then before him, or which were to be in the immediately succeeding period? In reply, we need but inquire, Was Jerusalem then, or has it since been, a "city of truth"—"the holy mountain?" Surely not. Note, moreover, a verse immediately following, where reference is plainly had to a restoration yet to be accomplished. "Thus saith the Lord of hosts, Behold I will save my people from the east country, and from the west country, and I will bring them, and they shall dwell in the midst of Jerusalem; and they shall be my people; and I will be their God, in truth and in righteousness." (8 : 7, 8.) That this passage has reference to a *yet* coming period, is again fully apparent from the closing verses of the chapter, where we find a description of scenes which, we think, no one will say have yet transpired. Thus, then, are the Jewish nation to be restored to the land promised to Abraham for a perpetual inheritance. And this restoration we find to be a favorite subject with the inspired seers. "It is, indeed," one well remarks, "the leading theme with the Jewish prophets. The original grant to Abraham is never lost sight of. It is the climax of every song of triumph, the key-note in reference to which every strain is set."[1]

It is worthy of special note, that to the hope of a literal restoration have the Jews, in all their wanderings, amid all their persecutions, under all the obloquy and contempt that have been so shamefully heaped upon them, clung with cherished fervency of spirit. So they read the prophecies given to their fathers; and the prospect comes to cheer their hearts, and to nerve them to more patient endurance of the wrongs inflicted upon them. "It is impossible," remarks Dr. Russell,[2] "not to be struck with the aspect of that grandest of all moral phenomena which is suspended upon the history and condition of the sons of Jacob. Nearly, if not quite as numerous as when David swayed the sceptre of the twelve tribes, their expectations are the same; and on whatever part of the earth's surface they have their abode, their eyes and their faith are all pointed in the same direction, to the land of their

[1] McNeile. [2] History of the Jews.

fathers, and the holy city where they worshipped. Although rejected by God and persecuted by man, they have not once, during eighteen hundred wearisome years, ceased to repose confidence in the promises made by Jehovah to the founders of their nation. And though the heart has often been sick and the spirit faint, they have never relinquished the hope of that bright reversion to the latter days, which is once more to establish the Lord's house on the 'top of the mountains,' and to make Jerusalem the glory of the whole world."

"The land of promise was the inheritance hoped for by Abraham and all his descendants; and that is the hope divinely begotten in the heart of every Jew; and wherever you find one of Abraham's scattered children, you find this hope occupying a prominent place in his bosom, and his eye and his affections are turning to that land of promise and of hope. He everywhere considers Judea as his proper country, and Jerusalem as his metropolitan city." "This recollection of country is unparalleled. The Jew has not lost it, and will not lose it, and he fondly transmits it to his posterity."[1]

Wilde, in his "Travels in Palestine," remarks: "Were I asked what was the object of greatest interest that I had seen, and the scene which made the deepest impression upon me, during my sojourn in other lands, I would say, that it was a Jew mourning over the stones of Jerusalem. And what principle, what feeling is it, it

[1] Harkness.

may be asked, that can thus keep the Hebrew, through so many centuries, still yearning towards his native city; still looking forward to his restoration and the coming of the Messiah? Hope. Hope is the principle that supports the Israelite through all his sufferings. With oppression for his inheritance, sorrow and sadness for his certain lot, the constant fear of trials, bodily pain and mental anguish; years of disgrace and a life of misery; without a country and without a home; scorned, robbed, insulted, and reviled; the power of man, and even death itself, cannot obliterate that feeling."

In Poland, when an independent nation, the Jews existed in large numbers, and were, it is said, formed into armies of the finest soldiers in Europe, and commanded by officers of their own nation. They were accustomed, frequently, to meet in their synagogues for fasting, humiliation, and supplication to the God of their fathers, with their faces towards Jerusalem and the ruins of their Temple, under a deep impression that the years of their long dispersion were hastening to a close; and that their God would soon turn again the captivity of his people.[1]

A lovely Jewish maiden, of superior mind, is represented as saying, a few years since, in anticipation of soon visiting Jerusalem, "Oh, that lovely place, whence I look for the revelation of Messiah, Ben David, my hope, and the hope of

[1] Thorp's Destinies of the British Empire.

Israel! Oh, that He were come, that all ungodliness might be turned away from Jacob! I shall see the lovely mountains which surround my city, as the Lord surrounds his people. I shall stand upon the holy spot where our Temple once reared its majestic front; a place wondrously beautiful and blessed, even in its present ruin. But how glorious will it be when Jehovah will gather us together again, with tender mercies, and, remaining with his people, be their King forever more! How glad shall I be to lay my lips against the stones which remain of the wall that surrounds the beloved city! With what rapture shall I breathe over them my humble prayer for succor and deliverance!"[1]

An influential journal at Leipsic, Germany, conducted by a learned Israelite, contained, a few years since, a stirring appeal to the Jews, with reference to their return to Palestine, in which the writer says, "The day of the Lord will appear: His wrath rests not forever on the unhappy seed of Abraham! For ages he has led us through the wilderness of privation and woe; but the trial is coming to an end. Already dawns the day of redemption from the east, from the land of our fathers, the loss of which we weep *with tears of*

[1] "Leila Ada" may be, as some are disposed to think, a work of mere fiction. But these, no one may doubt, are the throbbings of the spirit of many a Jew and Jewess in our day, who, realizing the sadness and privations of their disinherited condition, look with longing desire to the time when the "glorious things spoken of Zion" shall become actual verities.

blood. Our inheritance, rent from us by the destroying sword of the Romans; laid waste and desolate by inundations of Arabs, Seldshucks, Monguls, and Osmans, is expecting its lawful possessors to rise from annihilation to the eminence which David, the ruler of Jerusalem and Damascus, once conferred upon it. . . . . We have a country, the inheritance of our fathers, finer and more fruitful, better situated for commerce than many of the most celebrated portions of the globe. . . . . The power of our enemies is gone; the angel of discord has long since mown down their mighty hosts, and yet ye do not bestir yourselves, people of Jehovah! What hinders? Nothing but your own supineness! No Pharaoh will prevent our pilgrimage; no legions stop our course. . . . . Our probation was long in all countries, from the north pole to the south. People of Jehovah, raise yourselves from your thousand years' slumber! The rights of nations will never grow old. Take possession of the land of your fathers! Build the third time the Temple on Zion, greater and more magnificent than ever! Trust in the Lord, who has led you safely through the vale of misery thousands of years—He will not forsake you in your last conflict."[1]

For the very stones of their former Temple, this people, at Jerusalem, are said to cherish a sacred veneration. One converted from Judaism, remarks, "Their veneration is beyond descrip-

[1] Berg's History of the Jews.

tion. They never venture to approach the stones with shoes upon their feet. Prayers are offered before them on every Friday; and many of them are actually worn from kissing."[1]

At the base of the wall which supports the west side of the Temple area, is a place visited by every traveller at Jerusalem. It tells a sad tale, and presents a melancholy spectacle. It is the "wailing-place" of the Jews; and Dr. Thomson[2] assures us that no sight meets the eye more sadly suggestive, than this wailing of the Jews over the ruins of the Temple. This place is approached only by a crooked, narrow lane, terminating at a wall in a very contracted space, where, sheltered from observation, on the eve of their Sabbath, they meet to chant in mournful melody, with trembling lip and tearful eyes, the lamentations of their prophet: "Be not wroth very sore, O Lord, neither remember iniquity forever: behold! see! we beseech thee. We are all thy people. Thy holy cities are a wilderness, Jerusalem a desolation: our holy and beautiful house, where our fathers praised Thee, is burned with fire, and all our pleasant things are laid waste." And then,[3] with something like a dawn of hope, they cry, as an eye-witness declares,

"Lord, build—Lord, build—
Build thy house speedily.
In haste! In haste! Even in our days,
Build thy house speedily.

---

[1] Bib. Repository, 1840, p. 193. [2] The Land and the Book.
[3] Hugh McNeil's Lectures on the Jews.

"Lord, build—Lord, build—
Build thy house speedily.
In haste! In haste! Even in our days,
Build thy house speedily.
In haste! In haste! Even in our days,
Build thy house speedily."

Dr. Wolff gives the following affecting service, as used, some years ago, by the Karaite Jews,[1] at Jerusalem, the Rabbi and the people speaking alternately:

"R. On account of the palace which was laid waste,

P. We sit lonely and weep.

R. On account of the temple which was de stroyed,

P. We sit lonely and weep.

R. On account of the walls which are pulled down,

P. We sit lonely and weep.

R. On account of the precious stones which are burned,

P. We sit lonely and weep.

R. On account of the Priests who have stumbled,

P. We sit lonely and weep.

[1] The Karaites are a sect of the Jews, claiming, and not without reason, a great antiquity. They mainly differ from the larger body of the nation in the rejection of all traditions, and their rigid adherence to the letter of the law. At the time of Dr. Wolff's first visit to Jerusalem, he met them there in considerable numbers. At a later period, however, he found them reduced to a very few, and apparently soon to disappear from the holy city.

R. On account of our kings who have despised Him,

P. We sit lonely and weep.

R. We beseech Thee, have mercy upon Zion.

P. Gather the people of Jerusalem.

R. Make haste, O! Redeemer of Zion.

P. Speak to the heart of Jerusalem.

R. May beauty and majesty surround Zion,

P. And turn, with mercy, to Jerusalem.

R. Remember the shame of Zion.

P. Remember again the ruins of Jerusalem.

R. May the royal government shine on Zion.

P. Comfort those who mourn at Jerusalem.

R. May joy and gladness be found upon Zion.

P. A branch will come forth at Jerusalem."

Such are the feelings; such the bitter remembrance of their sins, which caused the Lord to withdraw his favor from them; such their lamentations, and such their fondly-cherished hopes. They do not live in expectation of being always thus scattered to the ends of the earth, a byword and hissing to every nation. With the prophecies of Moses, of Isaiah, of Jeremiah, of Ezekiel, and of Amos in their hands, they turn, with enduring hope, to Jerusalem and Palestine, feeling assured that as it was the promised inheritance of Abraham forever, so it will be theirs and their descendants', in very deed. And the providence of God seems to be keeping them not only in a state of expectancy, of hope, and longing desire, but in one of readiness to return; for it is a fact, to be noticed, that their possessions are usually such as may be easily taken with them, or readily converted into that which may be. But, comparatively, *very few* are to be found anywhere as large landed proprietors or agriculturists. Their intercourse with, and their relations to those among whom they live, are more like those of the wanderer, or mere sojourner, whose abode may be changed on the morrow. Having no dominion, no settled country, and usually no fixed property, there is nothing to detain them anywhere, when the favorable, set time for their restoration shall arrive.

The Rev. James Hamilton remarks,[1] "There is a city whose case is quite peculiar: captured, ravaged, burnt, razed to the foundation, dispeopled, carried captive, its deported citizens sold into slavery, and forbidden, by severest penalties, to visit their native seats again; though eighteen centuries have passed, and strangers still tread its hallowed soil, that city is still the magnet of many hearts, and awakens, from time to time, pangs of as keen emotion as when its fall was recent. Ever and anon, from all the winds of heaven, Zion's exiled children come to visit her, and with eyes weeping sore, bewail her widowhood. No city was ever honored thus; none else receives pilgrimages of affection from the fiftieth generation of its outcast people. None else, after centuries of dispersion, could at the first call, gather beneath its wings the whole of its wide, wandering family;

[1] "Destination of the Jews."

and none but itself can now be re-peopled with precisely the same race which left it nearly two thousand years ago. . . . . And now, why, when all other scattered nations mix and mingle—why is it that like naphtha in a fountain, or amber floating on the sea, this people, shaken hither and thither, are found, after all their tossings and jumblings, separate and immiscible? And why, again, when every other forsaken city, after an age or two, is forgotten by its people—why has Jerusalem such strong affinities for its outcast population, that the city refuses any other permanent inhabitants, and the old inhabitants refuse any other settled home?"

Thus have we clearly revealed to us, in the Scriptures of truth, the purposes of God in reference to this most remarkable people, touching at least the question of their actual restoration to the land of their forefathers. This fact is worthy of investigation by every one. But to the Christian it is one of commanding interest, because of its most intimate relation to other events immediately preceding, accompanying, or following it, involving the destinies of the world, and ushering in the momentous scenes which close the present, and commence a coming dispensation of divine glory, power, and grace.

CHAPTER III.

THE JEWS, CONTINUED.

RESTORATION NOT SPIRITUAL—RESTORATION AND CONVERSION DISTINCT—THEIR INIQUITY CULMINATING IN THE REJECTION OF THEIR MESSIAH, THE CAUSE OF ALL THEIR JUDGMENTS—THEIR PREDICTED REPENTANCE—TIME OF RESTORATION—"TIME" AND "FULNESS" OF THE GENTILES.

Glorious things are spoken of thee, O City of God.—Ps. 87: 3.

JERUSALEM is the subject of the Psalmist's fervent address. Of that city prophets had indeed spoken glorious things. Pleasant for situation, and magnificent in its buildings, Jerusalem was the joy of the whole earth. There was the royal residence of the kings of Judah; there was the Temple, and the Ark, and the glory; and the King of Heaven, dwelling in the midst of her. Her streets were honored with the footsteps of the Redeemer of men; there He preached, and there He died, and rose again; thither He sent down His spirit, and there He first laid the foundations of His Church. But at the time these latter events transpired, Jerusalem, as a city, had lost its glory. The Jews, who occupied it, and who still were permitted to worship where their fathers worshipped, had become a degenerate people; now subject to a Gentile power, to whom they were obliged to yield an ignominious tribute. And soon the measure of their iniquity being full, in the rejection of the Messiah, the doom of the city and the nation was sealed. On Olivet, the Redeemer, with the doomed city full in view, and looking over its once favored palaces, wept as He thought of its approaching desolation; and gave expression to those significant words which sealed the judicial blindness of a people from whom the things which made for their peace were now to be hidden.

In a few hours, that weeping, commiserating Jesus was a fully-rejected, persecuted, murdered man, hanging on the cross, just outside the walls of the city over whose doom He had so recently wept. The predicted judgments of heaven slumbered not; and the words of the Saviour spoken in the earlier period of his ministry, were hastening to their fulfilment; when the walls of that once glorious city should be laid prostrate, the Temple utterly destroyed, and all trodden down by Gentile feet; and when the people should be scattered among the nations of the earth.

We have seen how literally fulfilled have been the prophecies uttered not only by Jesus, but by holy, inspired seers of previous days, in reference to this remarkable people and the inheritance of their fathers, their city and their land. We have also seen with what feelings of special interest and of hope these Hebrews, in their world-wide dispersion, continue still to look towards "the City of the Great Prince." It is true that the nation anticipates the future coming of their Messiah at Jerusalem, at their restoration; and that advent so long looked for, with its accompanying and following events, is in their estimation to constitute the glorious things spoken of by David. But with no less interest may the Christian anticipate the full realization of all that the Psalmist meant. The Spirit of the living God who put these words into the mouth of His servant, looked far beyond all that should make Jerusalem of note, up to the offered sacrifice of Calvary. It embraced, we have reason to believe, more glorious things as connected with the City of God, than have yet transpired on earth. These have reference to the promised second advent of the Son of God: not to offer Himself up a second time, a sacrifice for sin, but to reign the ever blessed King of Zion—the predicted "David" of Jeremiah, of Hosea, of Ezekiel, and other prophets. Thither to the City of God, and to Palestine, will the scattered outcasts of the Jewish people be gathered when, the times of the Gentiles being fulfilled, the blindness which now, for centuries, has been upon their minds, shall mercifully be removed. As we have reason to believe, from the Scriptures of truth, that we, the descendants of Gentiles, are as deeply concerned as are the Jews, in the fulfilment of these predictions; so does it become us prayerfully to study the sacred Word touching these matters, that we may intelligently understand some of the glorious things spoken of the coming kingdom of the Redeemer.

There are still some things connected with the present condition and the restoration of the Jews, demanding consideration. No one, perhaps, who has examined the predictions already referred to, and kindred ones to be found on almost every page of the prophets, can doubt but that they are to have their special fulfilment in a time yet to come. There are, however, those who admit a future fulfilment of them, who think they are not to be literally verified, but that they are figurative, and admit of a spiritual interpretation. But as already remarked, it is impossible to see by what principle of correct interpretation of the prophecies, the already fulfilled, or now fulfilling predictions touching the condition of the Jews, should have been, and still continue to be, accomplished *most literally;* and the yet unfulfilled predictions, having reference to the same people, and given in immediate connection with the former, should not be as literally accomplished. The idea is, that the land specified by the prophets means the Christian Church; and that the return of the Jews to Jerusalem, and their restoration to Palestine, simply means their conversion to Christianity in this their state of dispersion, and their adoption into, or intimate union with, the converted Gentile nations.

But if this mode of interpreting prophecy, where there is no symbol and no figure, but a plain revelation, be adopted, then have we no certainty of the literal fulfilment of any prediction. No one doubts a literal season of prosperity and blessedness to the church, a literal second advent of Christ, a literal resurrection of the dead, a literal judgment, a literal experience of misery with the ungodly, and a literal state of heavenly blessedness for the people of God. But why not give a spiritual meaning to the predictions revealing *these* things, and thus change entirely the character of the events which the words appear so plainly to imply? Must not the same principles of interpretation be applied to both classes of subjects? But to make this still more evident, let us for a moment refer again to the "sure word of prophecy." We find, in Ezekiel, that the *restoration of the Jews to their land, and their conversion and sanctification*, are stated as two *distinct things*. In the 36th chap., 24th–28th vv, we read, "I will take you from among the heathen, and gather you out of all countries, and will bring you into your own land." There is one event definitely stated: "Then," at that time, "will I sprinkle clean water upon you, and ye shall be clean; . . . a new heart also will I give you, and a new spirit will I put within you; and I will take away the stony heart out of your flesh, and I will give you a heart of flesh." Here is another and a totally different thing, as definitely stated. The two cannot mean the same thing. Again he writes, "I will put my spirit within you, and cause you to walk in my statutes, and ye shall keep my judgments and do them." Here again is a definite statement. He proceeds,

"And ye shall dwell in the land which I gave to your fathers." The two things are as distinct in meaning as they are in statement. It is worthy of note, again, that their restoration is to be by a *migration or journey* from *many* countries to one. It is not a mere change from captivity to freedom, from spiritual blindness to light, to take place in the land of their dispersion. Some of the countries, moreover, from which they are to return, are specified, as is that to which they are to go. They are to come from the North and from the South, from the East and from the West, from Assyria and from Egypt, from Pathros and from Cush, and from the Islands of the Sea. The modes of their conveyance to Palestine are designated: Some are to be borne on arms, and some carried on horses, and mules, and in chariots; and some are to proceed by sea:—Is. 11:11; 49:22; 66:20, &c. Frequent allusions to these and other modes of conveyance are to be found in Isaiah. Are these specified modes of conveyance symbolical? Are we to understand by them various methods of bringing the Jewish people to Christ? What can a ride on the several animals specified, or in a chariot or litter, represent spiritually? What spiritual blessing can a voyage up the Mediterranean in a ship of Tarshish, symbolize? Is there any possible analogy between them and conversion? The question seems at once to suggest its appropriate and only answer.

But no longer to dwell on a point which must be sufficiently established, we proceed to remark, that *the rejection of the Jews, their present blindness, and wide dispersion, was because of their iniquity, culminating in their unbelief, and rejection of their Messiah.* The curses which were pronounced from Ebal, in the time of Joshua, were threatenings of judgments in case of disobedience. These judgments embraced their being scattered among the nations of the earth, and the endurance of the manifold evils to which they have been subjected for many centuries. And so the cause, definitely stated by later prophets, for the visitation of these sorrows, was their iniquity. This is admitted by the Jews themselves. They recognize the hand of a sin-avenging God in these evils. Thus spake the impassioned Hebrew preacher to his brethren:[1] "It was indeed a dark day in the history of our nation when we sinned against God. It was indeed a day portentous of calamity and untold sufferings. 'Let that day be darkness; let not God regard it from above; neither let the light shine upon it. Let darkness and the shadow of death stain it; let a cloud dwell upon it; let the darkness of the night terrify it.' No step could have been more fatal, no folly more disastrous, no act as pregnant with misery and suffering, as that of transgressing against the great and mighty God of Israel; and when God in His wrath averted His face from us, when the light of His gracious countenance no longer smiled upon us, fearful indeed was our punishment! God alone

[1] See page 26.

knows the enormity of our offence. God alone can tell how swift, how just, and how terrible has been the retribution."

A venerable Rabbi, longing for the appearance of the Messiah, a few years since, is said to have stood on an eminence on the coast of England. At his side was a beautiful girl, the daughter of the Rabbi's host. Pointing in the direction of Jerusalem, he said, "Yonder, my dear daughter, yonder lies the beloved city; *we know what excludes us from it;* and blessed be the Eternal! we know the remedy. Standing here, let us now stretch forth our hands in prayer. It may be, that the Holy One will hear, *and hearing, will forgive.*"

Thus is the conviction resting upon this people, that their existing calamities are the merited punishment for their sins; while yet they fail to see the crowning sin of all—that which filling up the measure to its fearful overflowing, immediately led to the full expression of the displeasure of their offended God. Their favorite prophet, Isaiah, in glowing language, reveals it; but they fail to understand his allusions: "He is despised and *rejected* of men, a man of sorrows and acquainted with grief, and *we hid*, as it were, *our faces from Him; He was despised, and we esteemed Him not.*" (53:3.) It was the rejection of their Messiah—the crucifixion of their prince—that filled up the cup of their iniquity. Paul, writing to the Thessalonians, says, "They both killed the Lord Jesus and their own prophets, and have persecuted us, . . . to fill up their sins always; for the wrath is come upon them to the uttermost." (1 Thess. 2:15, 16.) And in his Epistle to the Romans, he expressly states, "Because of unbelief they were broken off." (11:20.)

Another point deserving special notice is the predicted *repentance of the Jewish nation.* This is intimately connected with their restoration to their own land. They are not to be brought out from amid the nations of the earth as Jews; restored to Palestine as Jews, and there ever to continue as Jews, persisting in their iniquity, and in the rejection of Christ Jesus as their Messiah.

With deep repentance are they to mourn over, as they confess, their sinfulness. Read again in Deut.: "And it shall come to pass when all these things are come upon thee; the blessing and the curse; and thou shalt call them to mind among all the nations whither the Lord thy God hath driven thee, and shalt return unto the Lord thy God, and shalt obey his voice, according to all that I command thee this day, thou and thy children, with all *thy heart and with all thy soul;* that then the Lord thy God will turn thy captivity, . . . and gather thee from all the nations whither the Lord thy God hath scattered thee." (30:1–3.) Here the condition of their restoration is stated to be their calling these judgments to mind as the punishment of their iniquity and their consequent repentance. Again, in Leviticus, by the mouth of Moses, the Lord says: "If they shall confess their iniquity, and the iniquities of their fathers, with their trespass which they trespassed against me, and that they have also walked contrary unto me; . . . if then their uncircumcised hearts be humbled, and they then accept of the punishment of their iniquity; then will I remember my covenant with Jacob, and also my covenant with Isaac, and also my covenant with Abraham, will I remember, and I will remember the land." (26:40–42.) So by Hosea, He saith: "I will tear and go away: I will take away, and none shall rescue him: I will go and return to my place, *till they acknowledge their offence and seek my face.*" "Come, let us return unto the Lord, for he hath torn and he will heal us, he hath smitten and he will bind us up." (5:14, 15; 6:1.)

Thus, it appears that there is to be a national penitence for iniquity, immediately connected with their restoration. But that penitence is not to embrace a recognition of their sin in the rejection of Christ Jesus. *Such* repentance is, beyond all doubt, to be intimately connected with their ingathering from the nations; but it will be subsequent to their re-establishment in Palestine. Thus by their prophet Zechariah the Lord says: "Jerusalem shall be inhabited again in her own place, even in Jerusalem. . . . And I will pour upon the house of David and upon the inhabitants of Jerusalem the spirit of grace and of supplication; and they shall look upon me whom they have pierced; and they shall mourn for him as one mourneth for his only son, and shall be in bitterness for him, as one that is in bitterness for his first born." (12:6, 10.) Ezekiel also says: "I will take you from among the heathen and gather you out of all countries, and I will bring you into your own land. *Then* will I sprinkle clean water upon you, and ye shall be clean." (36 : 24, 25.)

When the humble acknowledgment of sin, and the apparent penitence of the recent fervent speaker in the Synagogue of New York, and that asserted of the venerable Rabbi in England, become the acknowledgment and the experience of the nation, we may expect the speedy fulfilment of the predicted restoration of Israel. And then shall the time and the fulness of the Gentiles be fulfilled.

Thus we are led briefly to inquire, *When shall these interesting predictions be fulfilled?* When will Israel's restoration come? and when the important events associated with it, the glorious things spoken of the City of God, transpire?

Purposing to examine more fully the subject of *the time* of the second advent in a subsequent chapter, we now desire to consider the restoration of the Jews merely in relation to the "*time*," and "the *fulness of the Gentiles*." What are we to understand by the "time," and "the fulness of the Gentiles," which being fulfilled, Jerusalem is no longer to be trodden down, nor is blindness any longer to be the condition of Israel; nor are the scattered people any longer to continue in their dispersion? "Blindness in part is happened to Israel, until the fulness of the Gentiles be come in." (Rom. 11 : 25.) "Jerusalem shall be trodden down of the Gentiles until the times of the Gentiles be fulfilled." (Luke 21:24.) Here is specified a definite period, the accomplishment of which insures the removal of the blindness from Israel. There can be no question but that these passages—one uttered by the Saviour himself, and the other penned by the inspired apostle—have reference to the same thing, "the times of the Gentiles," and "the fulness of the Gentiles." What are we to understand by them? Those who give a spiritual interpretation to these unfulfilled prophecies, teach that "the fulness of the Gentiles" means the complete, general conversion of the Gentile nations to the religion of the Cross. "The times," are those when the Gospel shall be spread throughout the world, and all the heathen nations, having abandoned their false religions and their abominations, shall be found the sincere worshippers of the only true and living God, within the pale of the Christian Church. It will be the full expansion and wide extension of the kingdom of Christ, embracing every kindred, and tribe, and people. But, it would seem, with one exception, and that is worthy of special notice. Every kindred, and tribe, and people are to be gathered into the kingdom, except the Jews, God's favored covenant nation; for *blindness* in part is happened to Israel *until* the *fulness* of the Gentiles be come in. If this be the correct understanding of the passage, then the whole Pagan and Antichristian world are to be converted, while yet the Hebrew people remain among them, in all their degradation, in their dispersion and their blindness; an idea refuted by the apostle in the immediate context, where he says, "If the fall of them be the riches of the world, and the diminishing of them the riches of the Gentiles, how much more their fulness." (Rom. 11:12.) If by their unbelief the Gentiles have the Gospel offered unto them, how much greater to the Gentiles will be the benefit of their restoration; "for if the casting away of them be the reconciling of the world, what shall the receiving of them be but life from the dead?" (Rom. 11:15.) "Life from the dead" to an astonished Gentile world! It is the assurance of greater, far richer blessings accruing to the nations, as a direct consequence of the restoration and conversion, or the reingrafting of the Jews, than had previously been enjoyed by them. This event, the change in the condition of the Jews, precedes the other, the experience of the richer blessings of the Gospel by the nations of the earth. So the Apostle clearly teaches. What are we, then, to understand by "the times and the fulness of the Gentiles," if it be not their general ingathering into the fold of Christ? Jerusalem has now been trodden down of the Gentiles for eighteen centuries. During this period, God has been gathering from among these nations a people to praise Him. Many such, in apostolic days, were made the subjects of the grace of God; and ever since (though at some periods to a greater extent than others) has the work of salvation been going on among those who, in distinction from the Jews, are known as Gentiles; embracing nominally Christian lands as well as Pagan nations. And this work is to continue until certain purposes of God shall be fulfilled, not in the thorough evangelization of these nations and the universal spread of the Gospel, constituting what we have been accustomed to call the Millennium; but rather in gathering in from these nations, and from, or "out of" every people, the election of his grace. Note now the words of St. James, delivered at the council of the apostles at Jerusalem, immediately following the address of Peter, the appointed messenger to the Gentiles. "Simeon hath declared how God, at the first, did visit the Gentiles, to take out of them a people for his name." Take out *from among* them a people. Such is the original. Not to make of them all a people, but to take out "from among" them a people. "And to this," continues St. James, "agree the words of the prophets, as it is written, After this"—After what? After a people shall be taken out from among them, "I will return and build again the tabernacle of David, which is fallen down; and I will build again the ruins thereof, and I will set it up; that the *residue* of men might seek after the Lord, and all the Gentiles upon whom my name is called." (Acts 15:14–17.) Here is declared the design and the issue of the mission to the Gentiles. It was to select from among them, or to take out of them, a people for the Lord. This selection has been going on ever since; for at no time, manifestly, has there been a universal gathering of any tribe, or nation, or kindred. And it is to continue yet for a time.

"After this." That is, after the selection, to its purposed fulness, shall be made by Christian effort to save the perishing, the Lord will return and build dilapidated Jerusalem; one object of which, as stated, is "that the *residue* of men might seek after the Lord, and all the Gentiles upon whom the name of the Lord shall be called."

Notice now the answer of Jesus to the question of the apostles, When the end should come? "This Gospel of the kingdom shall be preached in all the world for *a witness* unto all nations, and *then* shall the end come." (Matt. 24:14.) The destruction of the temple may have been "the end" in the unenlightened minds of the inquirers; but it had a much more important and far-reaching significancy and application in the mind of Him who gave the answer. It was to the end of the present dispensation, when these startling events, embracing the personal, visible advent of Christ, are to transpire, that the Redeemer mainly referred. So the words, in their connection, seem to imply. Thus we see that the preaching of the "Gospel of the kingdom in all the world for a *witness* unto all nations," had not reference merely to its promulgation to the then known world, in anticipation of the overthrow of the Jewish polity by the destruction of Jerusalem; but especially did it look through the then undefined period of mercy allotted to the Gentiles, stretching over many centuries. Thus, too, the angel whom St. John saw flying in the midst of heaven had the everlasting Gospel to preach unto them who dwell on the earth, and to every nation, and kindred, and tongue, and people, saying with a loud voice, "Fear God, and give glory to Him, for the hour of His judgment is come." (Rev. 14 : 7.) Intimating very clearly that the general proclamation of the Gospel was to be a warning and a witness to the people; and its being made to every nation, was to be the accomplishment of the purpose of God; and the commission to proclaim it would be the completion of the time, which would close with the hour of His judgment.

Thus it appears that "the times of the Gentiles" is that period of mercy granted to the nations, during which the Gospel of the kingdom is to be preached to them; and to be preached for a witness; and *when* fully preached, or preached to all nations and people; when all shall have heard of Christ; or, when what is meant, in the Divine purpose, by "for a witness," be fully accomplished, *then* shall come the long-promised period of Israel's release from captivity, their restoration to their fathers' land, and the removal of blindness from their eyes. During this period, however, a great and glorious work is to be accomplished among the Gentiles. As the Gentiles inherited the blessings when Israel was disinherited, or as they were "grafted in" when Israel was "cut off," so are multitudes of them to be brought to a saving knowledge of the Redeemer. During this period, the period now in progress, there are to be taken out from among the Gentiles "a people for his name." The elect people of God are all to be gathered into the fold, from these nations; a work worthy of the utmost missionary zeal and effort of the Church; and then, this gracious purpose being accomplished, and the Gospel having been preached to all the nations, the predicted time will be fulfilled, and Jerusalem shall be no longer trodden down of the Gentiles.

CHAPTER IV.

THRONE OF DAVID—THEOCRACY RESTORED.

THE THEOCRACY RESTORED—THE INCARNATE JEHOVAH THE LITERAL RULER—"MY KINGDOM NOT OF THIS WORLD"—THRONE OF DAVID—ENEMIES TO BE DESTROYED—THIS KINGDOM NOT THE GOSPEL DISPENSATION—"THY KINGDOM COME."

"*Thou shalt call His name JESUS. He shall be great, and shall be called the Son of the Highest; and the Lord God shall give unto Him the throne of His father David: and He shall reign over the house of Jacob forever, and of His kingdom there shall be no end.*"—LUKE 1 : 31–33.

THE literal restoration of the Jewish nation to the land of their fathers, is but one of a series of events of transcendent moment, which are the subjects of prophecy, and which deeply affect the interests of the Church and the destiny of our world. Are they to be as literally accomplished? Let us address ourselves to the inquiry, with the earnest prayer that the Spirit of all grace may guide us in our investigations, for it is most certainly a matter of great moment that we know the truth as God has revealed it.

A very important subject is suggested by the words of the angel, addressed to the virgin Mary (Luke 1:31–33), announcing the fact that she was to be the honored mother of the promised Messiah: "Thou shalt call His name Jesus," &c.

The subject suggested is,

The Restoration of the Theocracy.

"The form of government appointed for the tribes of Israel, and for the land given them of God, was, from the time of their exodus from Egypt, purely theocratical. God claimed for Himself the prerogatives of an absolute king over them. As an earthly king resides in his palace, among his people, gives his commands, punishes the transgressors of his laws, administers justice, and provides in various ways for the well-being of his empire; so God dwelt in the tabernacle, by the symbol of His glorious presence, above the Ark, where the Cherubim, with outstretched wings exhibited, as it were, the royal throne; and where rested, the shekinah or cloud glittering with fire."[1] Jehovah was subsequently virtually rejected when they demanded a king in imitation of the surrounding nations. From this is to be dated the commencement of that series of events which resulted in their rejection and their present dispersion. But that theocracy is, certainly in some form, to be re-established. Of this no one has a doubt; and if we understand the words of Gabriel aright, and the predictions of holy seers, that theocracy, or God-government, is here again, on this very earth, *literally* to exist. The Lord is

[1] Hon. Joel Jones.

again to occupy the throne; and here, in the person of the Redeemer—God incarnate—is He to reign over a ransomed, sanctified, and ever blessed people; "*for the Lord shall give unto Him the throne of His father David, and He shall reign over the house of Jacob forever.*"

The important question is, How are we to understand this prediction of Gabriel? Does he mean that Christ Jesus shall occupy a veritable throne—the throne of David—and as a visible king, personally reign here on earth over His Church? Or, are the words to be interpreted of a purely spiritual dominion in the hearts of believers?

The Millennium, according to some, is to consist of this latter or merely spiritual dominion. It is to be simply a period when the hearts of all will be brought into submission to the will of God; when all that is wrong in the existing governments of earth shall be rectified; when every system of delusion, and superstition, and error shall come to an end, and righteousness shall universally prevail; a period of peace, and prosperity, and joy, to be *followed* by the visible second advent of the Son of God in judgment. It is thought that the idea of this spiritual dominion exhausts this prophecy of Gabriel and that of others equally explicit.

Of a spiritual reign of Christ over the hearts of his people no one doubts. But in connection with this, the Scriptures seem most clearly to reveal the fact, that this season of millennial glory is to be ushered in, and not to be followed by the literal coming of the glorious Son of God; here, personally and literally, to reign, the Prince of Zion. Both views cannot be correct. It is of importance to learn, if we can, which is in accordance with the teachings of the word of God. Let us examine the subject without prejudice, and with the docility of children desirous of instruction.

Christ is revealed most clearly in the Bible as sustaining the threefold character of Prophet, Priest, and King. As such, He was the subject of prophecy. Personally, literally, has He appeared as our *Prophet*, the great and blessed Teacher of the Church, as here, on earth, "He spake as never man spake." Personally, literally has He also appeared as our great efficient *Priest*, as here, on earth, He offered up the atoning sacrifice for a lost world. Has He personally, literally appeared as *King?* Ancient prophets spoke of Him in His twofold condition. They clearly predicted the advent of a lowly sufferer—a persecuted, rejected, murdered one. Of His humiliation as a man of sorrows they distinctly prophesied. But no less clearly did they exhibit His regal dignity. He was spoken of as Israel's Deliverer, Prince, and King; as one who was to reign; to have a universal dominion, and a kingdom that should never end. He was to be upon His throne, the Sovereign over the nations. All this was as clearly foretold as was His lowly condition as a rejected man of sorrows. The idea of His *royal* character was seized by the nation of the Jews; and not mindful of the fact that He must, according to prediction, first be an humble, suffering man; and clothing their Messiah with all the dignity, and power, and glory of a king, they rejected the lowly Nazarene who claimed to be their Deliverer. Had the Jews received Jesus as their Messiah, we have reason to believe that the kingdom of Christ would then have been set up, and Jesus would then have received the throne of David. The kingdom did come nigh unto them. It was "within" or "among" them. It was the burden of the Baptist's and the Saviour's preaching. The great error of the Jews was in losing sight of all that the prophets had predicted in reference to a *suffering* Messiah, and in looking, exclusively, at what was said of Him in His *regal* condition as Israel's promised King.

The prophecies in reference to the Saviour's lowly suffering condition have been all literally fulfilled. Have they been, or are they yet to be, as literally fulfilled in reference to His reigning as King upon the throne of David? His predicted prophetic and sacerdotal offices have been all literally verified here on earth, so far as they could be verified below. Is His royal office to fail, or is it to receive an entirely different verification, even a spiritual or figurative one? Is there not suggested here a strong presumption that Christ Jesus is yet to be the literal, personal, visible Ruler of His people; that He is to set up His throne, and here to reign? But the mention of this thought may suggest to some mind a declaration of the Saviour, which would seem of itself to settle the question—"My kingdom is *not of this world.* If my kingdom were of *this world*, then would my servants fight, that I should not be delivered to the Jews; *but now is my kingdom not from hence.*" (John 18:36.) Christ's kingdom is not of this world. The truthfulness of the Saviour's words is not to be called in question. But what does he mean to teach? The phrase translated "not of this world," is literally "not from or out of this world;" implying that this kingdom is not of human origin, but heavenly, or of or from heaven, and not of or from man. Jesus once propounded the question: "The baptism of John, whence was it; from heaven or of men?" (Matt. 21:25.) This inquiry has undoubted respect to the origin of his baptism. Is it heavenly, or is it human? Is it of or from heaven? or is it of or from men? Now note, the word is the same in the other passage, "of this world," and, obviously, refers to the *origin* of the kingdom. It is not of this world any more than was the baptism of John of men. It was heavenly, and not to be established by the might of armies in the flesh, or upheld by human power. "If it were," said Jesus, "then would my servants fight, that I should not be delivered to the Jews." In a very important sense is the kingdom of Christ not of this world; a sense which is no way at variance with the position, that He will literally appear to reign on the throne of David. Krummacher says of this passage: "He does not deny that He came to establish a kingdom. He only repels the groundless suspicion of His having intended to overthrow the existing authorities, and to establish a new political state."

As intimately connected with this subject of a restored theocracy, it is of interest to note the proceedings of Jehovah at the death of Saul, the king granted to the rebellious people in answer to their special request, that they might have a regal government, to correspond to the nations around them. It might be supposed that their experience under his administration would lead them to desire to return to the immediate supervision of the Lord, and that God would, after permitting them to try their chosen experiment, restore again the administration of the Judges. Instead of this, however, and without a renewal of the demand on the part of the people, we find Him, by a very special arrangement, selecting another king for them. And what demands our marked attention is, that He was graciously pleased to enter into a covenant with David, the selected Prince, embracing most important provisions and glorious assurances.

This covenant has a very special bearing upon the theocracy yet to be established. The assurance of the prophet was that the successors of David upon the throne should be of his seed, and that his kingdom should be established. This was literally fulfilled. For although because of the sins of Solomon the kingdom was divided by the revolt of the ten tribes, yet the family of

David ruled over Judah until the Babylonish captivity in the family of David. But this further assurance was given: "Thine house and thy kingdom shall be established *forever*. . . . . Thy throne shall be established *forever*." (2 Sam. 7:16.) This promise became the theme of grateful remembrance and of praise with David as he made mention of the faithfulness of the Lord, who declared, "I have made a covenant with My chosen; I have sworn unto David My servant. Thy seed will I establish *forever*, and build up thy throne to *all generations*. . . . My covenant will I not break. . . . His seed shall endure forever. And his throne . . . shall be established forever." (Ps. 89.) At the captivity, the authority and kingdom of David was interrupted: the throne was vacated; and thus has it continued unto the present hour. Has the Lord then falsified his word? Has He indeed violated a covenant which He declared should never be broken? If that throne is not to be restored; if David's kingdom and rule are not to be re-established, then must the covenant fail. But hear the words of Peter on the day of Pentecost, as he expounds the meaning of the covenant. "God had sworn with an oath to him [David], that of the fruit of *his loins, according to the flesh*, he would raise up *Christ to sit on his throne*." (Acts 2:30.) And so said Gabriel: "God shall give unto Jesus the throne of David, and He shall reign over the house of Jacob *forever*, and of His kingdom there shall be no end." This is all to be literally fulfilled, to the glory of Jehovah's truthfulness and honor, at the coming of the Son of man. A fact which it is our purpose to attempt to make manifest.

In the 37th chapter of Ezekiel, where, after the predicted union of the tribes, represented by the significant emblem or symbol of the joining together of the two sticks, it is said: "Behold, I will take the children of Israel from among the heathen, . . . and I will make them one nation upon the mountains of Israel; and *one king* shall be king *to them all;* . . . and *David* My servant shall be king over them. . . . And they shall dwell in the land that I have given unto Jacob; . . . and they shall dwell therein forever; and My servant *David* shall be their Prince forever." All this has reference to the establishment of the Hebrew people in Palestine, with Jerusalem as their restored metropolis. How similar to this declaration of the prophet is the assurance of Gabriel to Mary? "The Lord shall give to Him the throne of David, and He shall reign over Jacob." We have seen that the restoration must be a literal restoration; and by what admitted law of interpretation are we permitted to say that the kingdom is a spiritual and not a literal kingdom? If one be literal, does it not appear that the other, mentioned in immediate connection, must also be? The predicted King is, here and elsewhere, called David, and the throne to be occupied is the throne of David. By which is obviously meant a descendant of David; and none other but Jesus the incarnate Son of God is designated by the term, as the words of Gabriel explicitly affirm. Jeremiah, in the 23d chapter of his prophecies, writes: "Behold the days come, saith the Lord, that I will raise unto David a righteous *Branch;* and a *King* shall reign and prosper, and shall execute judgment and justice in the earth. In his days Judah shall be saved, and Israel shall dwell safely; and this is His name whereby he shall be called, THE LORD OUR RIGHTEOUSNESS."

Isaiah declares: "Unto us a Child is born; unto us a Son is given; and the *government* shall be upon His shoulder. . . . Of the increase of His government and peace there shall be no end; upon the throne of David and upon his kingdom, to order it and to establish it with judgment and with justice, from henceforth even forever." (Is. 9: 6, 7.) That the King spoken of in these and the many passages of the prophets, of which these are quoted but as specimens, is none other than the anticipated Messiah, is beyond all question. The angel, we again remark, declares it to be so; for he assures Mary that to *Jesus* the promised throne should be given, the throne of David, and that He should reign over the house of Jacob forever. Isaiah again declares; "The Lord shall reign in Mount Zion, and in Jerusalem, and before His ancients, gloriously." (24: 23.) Thus is there to be a kingdom. This no one may doubt. And the only inquiry is, will that kingdom be a literal kingdom? Will Christ, in very deed, personally occupy the literal throne of David? Or, is it all to be understood as a spiritual reign in the hearts of God's people? Is this language, so plain and emphatic in its import, met by such an understanding of it? David's throne was a literal throne. His kingdom was not a spiritual kingdom in the hearts of others. He lived and reigned over subjects in the flesh, personally, visibly present to them. And this throne is to be given to Jesus. It is the throne of David. Hear now again, and more fully, the words of Peter, on the memorable day of Pentecost, and mark them carefully: "Men and brethren, let me freely speak unto you of the patriarch David. . . . . Therefore, being a prophet, and knowing that God had sworn with an oath to him, that, of the fruit of *his loins*, according to *the flesh*, He would *raise up* Christ to sit on his throne. He seeing this before, spake of the *resurrection* of Christ." (Acts 2: 29–31.) Here was declared to be an intimate connection between the *occupancy* of the throne of David and the *resurrection of the body of Jesus*. It is the humanity of Christ that is spoken of; and His humanity, He who was "of the loins of David according to the flesh," was to be *raised* up, that He might sit upon His throne. Will this admit of a spiritual interpretation? Christ reigns by His Spirit in the hearts of His people; but His *resurrected humanity* is to have a throne; and must it not have a different throne than the hearts of men, whereon to sit? That there is to be a literal kingdom over which Christ Jesus is to rule, appears, moreover, from the declarations of Daniel.

Nebuchadnezzar, the king of Babylon, had a dream of a great image, the head whereof was of fine gold; his breast and his arms of silver; his belly and thighs of brass; his legs of iron; his feet, part of iron and part of clay. These several parts represented four successive kingdoms, as Daniel himself assures us. They were those of Babylon, the Medo-Persian, the Grecian, and the Roman. These arose, one after the other, each on the ruins of its predecessor. The fourth, or the Roman kingdom, was the last. That, according to Daniel's interpretation, being part of potter's clay and part of iron, should be a divided kingdom, as symbolized by the toes of the image. That kingdom was divided, and remains in its divided condition to this day, mainly on the continent of Europe. All this is a matter of absolute history. Shall this fourth empire continue ever; or is it to share the fate of its predecessors? Mark the prophecy. Said Daniel to the king: "Thou sawest till that a stone was cut out, without hands, which smote the image upon his feet of iron and clay, and brake them to pieces. . . . And they became like the chaff of the summer threshing-floor, and the wind carried them away, that no place was found for them. *And the stone, which smote the image, became a great mountain, and filled the whole earth.*" (2:31–35.) Now what is the meaning of all this? The prophet himself answers: "In the days of these kings,"—the kings of this divided empire, the very state of things now existing—"In the days of these kings shall *the God of heaven set up a kingdom*, which shall never be destroyed. And the kingdom shall not be left to other people: but it shall break in pieces, and consume all these kingdoms, and it shall stand forever." (v. 44.) And what is the character of this last kingdom which is to supplant and destroy the rest? Is it a spiritual kingdom? It is far from being so stated. But if it be such, by what law of interpretation, we again inquire, are we led to this conclusion? "It is not of this world," we may be told. Truly, it is not; for the stone which overthrew the image, and became, in the prophet's sight, a mountain, was cut out "*without hands.*" It was not of or from this world. Its origin was divine. The four previous monarchies were literal, veritable monarchies, having their literal existence on earth, as their prophetic history foretold, and the providence of God subsequently made manifest.[1] They had their literal rulers or kings, who occupied the throne; their literal government and defined territories. Each had its subjects, over whom it reigned, and enemies whom it conquered and destroyed. All these were upon the earth in visible form, succeeding one another, and each becoming more powerful than its predecessor. If, then, four of these monarchies were literal, as is well known from history that they were, and also from the still existing remains of the fourth, under the emblem of the ten toes, what can the inference be but that the fifth shall be of the same

[1] Harkness.

nature? Why understand the four to be literal kingdoms, but the fifth spiritual in its nature? It surely will be a kingdom with its visible organization, its visible Ruler, its subjects, and territory, and yet "a kingdom whose foundations are laid by infinite wisdom and in absolute righteousness; divine in its origin, divine in its principles, divine in its laws and government. But who is to be the ruling Prince, the Sovereign of this new kingdom? Again, Gabriel answers the question in his message to the virgin mother." It is JESUS. Daniel also solves the problem. In the vision of the four beasts, designed to symbolize the same great truths which the vision of Nebuchadnezzar did, the prophet says: "I saw in the night visions, and behold, one like the *Son of man* came, with the clouds of heaven, and came to the Ancient of days, and they brought Him near before Him. And there *was given Him dominion, and glory, and a kingdom, that all people, nations, and languages should serve Him.* His dominion is an everlasting dominion which shall not pass away; and His kingdom that which shall not be destroyed." (Dan. 7:14.) There is nothing in this statement to imply a mere spiritual dominion in the hearts of God's people. That such a dominion exists, and ever will exist, is a blessed truth. This spiritual kingdom is the entire subjection of man's spirit to the will of God. But is this all? The whole man is to be subject to Christ; the material, the glorified body, as well as the spiritual part of his being. And provision is made for this in the *resurrection* state, and in that kingdom over which Christ is to reign. This kingdom cannot be the Gospel dispensation, because the prophecy calls for an absolute, literal, and visible kingdom, which this dispensation is not. "The rule of the Gospel in the heart," as William Newton well and forcibly remarks, "is altogether a spiritual rule. It has nothing to do with visible dominions. It sits not down in the high places of power. It sways not the sceptre. It wields not the sword. It lays no scheme for the overthrow of thrones. *It is not, therefore, the kingdom pointed out by the prophet.* Of the four kingdoms which have already come, the second displaced the first; the third overturned the second; and the fourth built up its throne on the ruins of the three which had gone before it. So the kingdom of God is to take the place of all other kingdoms, and *as a kingdom* to fill the whole earth!" It is to be done, remember, by breaking in pieces and consuming all these kingdoms, and driving them away as the wind does the chaff of the threshing-floor; whereas the rule of the Gospel is, "Peace on earth, good will to men." It has nothing to do with the imagery of destruction, with garments rolled in blood; with the onset of armies and the putting down of thrones. Its mission is to tell the story of the crucified. Its plea is "the love of Christ." Its weapons are not carnal, but spiritual; and all its conquests are wrought by "the sword of the Spirit, which is the word of God." It is scarcely possible to conceive of a contrast greater than that pointed out between its triumphs and those of the kingdom of which the prophet speaks.

You observe, that it is "the Stone" which smote the image on its feet. Now as Christ is this stone, this *smiting is clearly to be done by Him.* It is not a spiritual smiting by His truth. *That* never breaks and subdues kingdoms, and scatters them as chaff before the wind. Christ Himself, in "the brightness of His coming," and not His truth, "will be the destruction of His banded foes. Nothing less than this will satisfy the demands of the prophetic word."

The advent of the predicted King, to whom is to be given the throne of David, it is repeatedly declared, will be attended with the signal destruction of his persistent enemies. Read in the second Psalm, where David says, as he anticipated coming events, "Why do the heathen rage, and the people imagine a vain thing; the kings of the earth set themselves, and the rulers take counsel together against the Lord and against his Anointed. . . . He that sitteth in the heavens shall laugh. The Lord shall have them in derision. Then shall He speak unto them in His wrath, and vex them in His sore displeasure. *Yet have I set My King upon My holy hill of Zion.* Ask of me, and I shall give Thee the heathen for Thine inheritance, and the uttermost parts of the earth for Thy possession. Thou shalt break them with a rod of iron. Thou shalt dash them in pieces like a potter's vessel." (2 : 1–9.) Such is the language employed by Jehovah to Him who is to sit as King upon the holy hill of

Zion. Is this breaking of enemies with a rod of iron, this dashing of them to pieces like a potter's vessel, figurative language meant to express the peaceful influences of the truth in overcoming the prejudices of men, and bringing them under the spiritual dominion of the Gospel? Is it not doing violence to language thus to understand the words? The heathen, or the nations, are to be given to Christ as an inheritance, and the uttermost parts of the earth for a possession.

But it is not to be accomplished, it would appear, by the gradual peaceful conquests of the truth. The *stone* is to *smite* the *image* and *destroy* it. Christ Jesus is to break in pieces all the combinations of His enemies, by an absolute and sudden and remediless destruction. And all this is to be effected at His predicted second coming.

It is worthy of note that the restoration of the dispersed Hebrew people is declared to be amid startling revolutions and signal judgments upon the enemies of God.[1] That restoration and these judgments will be when the throne of David is given to *Jesus*, or when the Lord shall set His King upon His holy hill of Zion—when He shall come in the clouds of heaven, as was declared by the celestial messengers on the Mount when Jesus ascended up on high. Then will the Theocracy be established. Jehovah, in the person of the incarnate Redeemer, will reign over the house of Jacob, and over a ransomed earth; for great voices shall be heard in heaven, saying, "The king-

[1] See chap. 6.

doms of this world are become the kingdoms of our Lord and of His Christ;" or, as is thought to be the more correct rendering, the *kingdom*, the rule or dominion, of this world is become the kingdom or dominion of our Lord and of His Christ. (Rev. 11:15.)

For the *advent* or *coming* of that kingdom we are directed by the Saviour ever to pray, "*Thy Kingdom come.*" A spiritual dominion is *now* exercised over the hearts of believers. He rules and reigns among His people. He is ever with them; ever with His Church, in this present dispensation. But the kingdom for which we are to pray is a kingdom *yet to come.* "Thy kingdom *come,*" when the will of God shall "be done on earth, even as it is done in heaven." A period surely not yet arrived.

Thus this spiritual dominion, the kingdom now existing, and which has existed since the first regenerated soul became a subject of the grace of Christ, appears not to be the kingdom here referred to; nor that of which Gabriel spoke; nor that which Ezekiel in prophetic vision saw; nor that which was the theme of Isaiah's glowing utterances as he predicted a season of universal blessedness here on earth. The advent of that kingdom will be the commencement of the Millennium. The administration of that kingdom under Christ will be the blessedness of that season of righteousness. And it will be ushered in by the second advent of our Immanuel Prince. Let us then earnestly pray, "*Thy Kingdom* COME."

CHAPTER V.

PRE-MILLENNIAL ADVENT.

ERROR OF THE JEWS — A MILLENNIUM — INTRODUCED BY CHRIST AT HIS COMING—AND NOT THE RESULT OF THE GRADUAL SPREAD OF TRUTH AND RIGHTEOUSNESS—SLOW PROGRESS OF THE GOSPEL — LESSONS OF PROVIDENCE — TEACHINGS OF THE SCRIPTURES — THE GOSPEL TO BE PREACHED FOR A WITNESS—ELECTION OF GRACE.

And he added and spake a parable, because he was nigh to Jerusalem, and because they thought that the kingdom of God should immediately appear. He said, therefore, A certain nobleman went into a far country to receive for himself a kingdom, and to return.—LUKE 19 : 11, 12.

JESUS, as He uttered these words, was at Jericho, on His way to Jerusalem, there, in a few days, to be crucified. He was attended not only by His immediate disciples, but by a large multitude, who, attracted by His wonderful works, and animated by their cherished hopes, with joyous acclamations followed Him. Different were the greetings He now received from those which were uttered by many of the same persons a few hours subsequently. Now, they hailed Him as their Prince; then, they clamored for His punishment as an impostor. Now, they cried, "Blessed be the king who cometh in the name of the Lord; peace in heaven and glory in the highest." Then, they cried; "Crucify him! crucify him!" The Jews were anticipating the establishment of the kingdom predicted by their prophets. Their Messiah was to be a king, and He was to have a veritable kingdom. They, in their subjection to Gentile rulers, longed for deliverance; and, as has been remarked before, losing sight of the priestly office of the Promised One, in the execution of a part of which He was to be an humble sufferer, they thought solely of His royal dignity, as their promised King and Deliverer. And believing at this time that Jesus was He of whom the prophets had spoken, and for whom they were looking, they persuaded themselves that He was now on His way to Jerusalem, the predicted metropolitan city, there to erect His throne and commence His reign; "for He was nigh to Jerusalem, and they thought that the kingdom of God should immediately appear."

Their expectation that such a kingdom was in very deed to be established, was not their error. In this they were correct. Their nation had believed it; for inspired men had predicted it. And the Saviour admits the correctness of their belief in the very parable which He uttered to correct what was their mistake, namely, that the kingdom should *immediately* appear. They considered it as near at hand, indeed to begin now, on His entering Jerusalem. Said the Divine teacher; "A certain nobleman went into a far country, to receive for himself a kingdom, and to return;" to return, most obviously, to establish the kingdom thus given him. The whole parable was designed to correct their error, and to impress upon them the importance of improving the talents intrusted to them, in anticipation of the account to be rendered when the nobleman should return with his kingdom.

This introduction to the parable suggests, *first*, a kingdom to be established; *second*, the return of the nobleman; *third*, the relation of his advent to the kingdom; or, to drop the phraseology and imagery of the parable,—

1. THE MILLENNIUM. 2. THE SECOND ADVENT OF CHRIST; AND, 3. THE RELATION OF THE SECOND ADVENT TO THAT PERIOD OF PREDICTED BLESSEDNESS.

We consider, *first*, THE PREDICTED MILLENNIUM, "*a Kingdom to be received.*"

The term Millennium, although not used in the Scriptures, is derived from the 20th chapter of the Revelation, where it is predicted that Satan should be bound a *thousand years*,[1] and that the pious dead—the risen saints—should reign with Christ during these thousand years. It is admitted that there is in store for the people of God a season of prosperity and blessedness, such as the world has never known. The very term, Millennium, is not simply expressive of a period of a thousand years; but common usage now gives it the import of a period of unprecedented felicity,

[1] Mille Annorum.

without reference to the Scripture season or to duration. That the Church is justified in the expectation of such a time, no one doubts. It was the all-animating theme of the prophets of old, and its anticipated advent has been the subject of prayer, and the consolation of the saints in every generation. The god of this world is not always to rule; nor is iniquity always to abound; nor will the misery and wretchedness, the oppression and violence, the corruption and ungodliness of the nations continue forever. The time will come when a gladsome voice will be heard in Zion, saying; "Arise, shine, for thy light is come, and the glory of the Lord is risen upon thee. . . . . Violence shall no more be heard in thy land, wasting nor destruction within thy borders; but thou shalt call thy walls Salvation and thy gates Praise. . . . . The Lord shall be thy everlasting light, and the days of thy mourning shall be ended. Thy people, also, shall be all righteous. They shall inherit the land forever." (Is. 60:1, 18, 20, 21.) Nor will this season of rejoicing be limited to the experience of restored Israel, to whom it was originally assured. For it will be a time when the kingdom or dominion of *this world* will have become the kingdom of Christ. Such is the period as foretold; as anticipated; as prayed for. All rejoice in the prospect of it. The Church is anxiously, yet joyfully waiting for it. Every one believes it who believes the Bible.

A millennium of glory, of peace, and righteousness, is then to be the experience of our earth.

That millennium is the kingdom of Christ. His administration of the kingdom is to be the blessedness of the millennium. But if this be the unquestioned opinion of the Church, so is there as certain an expectation of a personal second advent of the Son of man *at some period.* The first advent of the Messiah was not more clearly and fully foretold by the Old Testament seers than is the second. But it is, perhaps, more especially revealed in the Scriptures of the New Testament. "Enoch, the seventh from Adam, prophesied, saying; Behold! the Lord cometh with ten thousand of his saints." (Jude 14.) The angelic messengers declared to the astonished disciples, on the mount of ascension; "This same Jesus which is taken up from you into heaven shall *so come in like manner* as ye have seen Him go into heaven." (Acts 1:11.) "Hereafter," said Jesus Himself, "shall ye see the Son of man sitting on the right hand of power, and coming in the clouds of heaven." (Matt. 26:64.) And St. Paul affirms; "The Lord Himself shall descend from heaven with a shout, with the voice of the archangel, and with the trump of God." (1 Thess. 4:16.) But not to multiply passages, of which the Bible is full, we remark, that a plain, undoubted reference to a literal, personal second coming of Christ Jesus to our earth occurs not less than 120 times in the New Testament Scriptures. It is spoken of as a "*revelation of Christ;*" an "*appearing,*" or *manifestation;* a "*coming;*" a "*descending;*" the "*presence;*" "*the day of the Lord;*" "*the day of His coming.*"

Thus it is clearly predicted, that He who was once on earth, a man of sorrows, the rejected Nazarene, will revisit the scenes of His humiliation. But He will come the second time on a very different mission from that on which He came at first. He is the Nobleman who has gone into a far country "to receive a kingdom, and to return." Am I told that He will, indeed, come at the end of the world—the end or destruction of our globe—in judgment, to reward his saints and to inflict punishment on the ungodly, and that all this will occur at the close of the predicted millennium—when it is thought, by those who hold this opinion, that this world's history will end—time's drama be positively finished? This is the important question demanding now our careful examination. Christ is certainly to appear. Will His coming be before or after the thousand years? Will He come to spend a brief period in judgment, destroy the earth, and then pass away again? Or, will He come before the millennium, here to establish His kingdom, here personally to reign, His very presence and dominion constituting millennial glory? Will He come, with His saints, to *introduce* this period of righteousness? or, will it be brought about by agencies now in operation? Will it be the result of the gradual extension of the Gospel, until all nations shall be subdued by its peaceful, saving influence? Shall the thousand years of paradisaical purity and happiness, during which He is to reign, precede or follow the second advent? For an answer to these inquiries we may consult both the teachings of Divine Providence and the lessons of Scripture.

I. *The teachings of the Providence of God.*

What says the history of centuries past, and what the present aspect of our world, in reference to the coming millennium being the result of the gradual spread of Gospel truth by instrumentalities now employed? What reason have we to believe that the nations of the earth are thus to be won to Christ, leading to a spiritual reign universally, in the hearts of men? The Gospel is to be preached "for a witness" to the nations, or for a testimony against wickedness, and for judgment to come; a testimony or witness of gracious offers of reconciliation, the preaching of which will result in multitudes being made the subjects of the grace of God; and who will thus be taken out from among the nations to be a people "for His name." But will anything more than this be accomplished? Will the whole world be in this way evangelized, and the nations made the willing subjects of the Prince of Peace? How does the providence of God respond to this inquiry?[1]

Upwards of eighteen hundred years has the Gospel been proclaimed. We can trace the history of its results to the present hour; and it is a fact beyond the possibility of refutation, that while some have been truly converted, wherever the truth has been made known, the rejecters of the Gospel have ever very greatly outnumbered those who have savingly accepted it. We speak of the

[1] See chap. 8 for further remarks on this subject.

advance of the Gospel from generation to generation; of its spread from country to country; of nations becoming nominally Christianized. But does it amount to anything more than that the Gospel is merely a *witness* to the nations? For where is the instance to be found, even in nominally Christian nations, where the vast, overwhelming majority are not confessedly the enemies of the Most High?

The professed people of God have always been greatly in the minority, and the body of true believers always a "little flock." It has been estimated that *pure* Christianity, after eighteen centuries, prevails even nominally with only about 80,000,000, out of the vast population of the globe; of these 80,000,000 there are but 15,000,000 who *profess* to be the disciples of Christ; as appears from the "*communion statistics*" of all the various branches of the Church throughout the world. And this number must, we fear, be very considerably reduced, if we seek the truly regenerated subjects of the grace of God. But making it as large as Christian charity can possibly warrant, the number of those who belong to the true spiritual fold of the Redeemer is, confessedly, most lamentably small. It is a little, a very little flock. If the world is to be converted by the gradual advance of Gospel truth, should we not expect to find a result far different from this after a lapse of more than 1800 years? It is a sad lesson the providence of God is teaching us. Sad as respects the moral picture of the race, and sad as respects the anticipations of many; and yet a lesson which should lead to a serious inquiry as to the revealed purposes of the Most High.

Dr. Duff, whose praise is in all the churches, says: "Notwithstanding all the efforts to propagate the Gospel, there are more heathen upon the earth now, than there were in the days of our Saviour." We sometimes hear of aggressions upon Romanism—of its waning power. There is, indeed, in these last days, some modifications of the external relations of this system of iniquity, and some change of policy and of tactics. But will not facts justify the statement of Macaulay, the historian, who says; "During the past 250 years, Protestantism has made no conquests worth speaking of. Nay, we believe, as far as there has been a change, that change has been in favor of the Church of Rome."

Look at this subject in the light of the most favored portions of Christendom, and what is the result? In the city of London, the metropolis of the most Christian nation of the Old World, the great fountain-head of benevolent enterprise, the provision which is made for church accommodation, or church sittings, falls 1,888,000[1] below the actual population, these being but 800,000 in a population of 2,688,000! And no one need be informed that these sittings are not all occupied. It may be safely estimated that not more than two-thirds of them are habitually filled; so that but about 520,000 are attendants upon the means

[1] See Newcomb's "Harvest and Reapers."

of grace. Thus in that one city, the source and centre of moral influences greater than any other of the eastern world, there are 2,168,000 who need to feel the power of Gospel truth as much as do the millions of Pagan lands! These are startling facts for the nineteenth century of the Christian dispensation. But let us come nearer home. In thirteen of the principal cities of the United States, with a population, a few years since, of 2,048,785, church sittings were provided but for 852,436, leaving a deficiency of accommodations of 1,200,000. And according to the above estimate of actual occupants of the sittings provided, the number of habitual neglecters of the means of grace, and who, as a class, are, if not in their social habits, yet in their religious character, semi-heathens, is not less than 1,480,000 out of a population of 2,048,000, living in the very heart of Gospel influences.

In 1854, an estimate was made of the result of missionary labor in heathen countries. So far as could be ascertained, there were connected with Christian congregations, 1,572,000. Comparing this number with those who are living in the city of London without giving any heed to the subject of religion, we find the latter to exceed the former by 596,000! Five hundred and ninety-six thousand more persons who are habitual neglecters of religion in that great city of Christian enterprise, than are to be found numbered among the nominal converts from heathenism, of all evangelical denominations! It may be that some of the above estimates are not exact. We do not claim that they are. All we need, in order to show what is the power of Gospel truth in this wicked world, as touching these particular localities, is to know that the estimates are proximately correct.

But let us look a little further. Nowhere, perhaps, has the Gospel been more fully, more faithfully, and more successfully proclaimed than in our own favored New England States, the early home of the Puritan fathers.[1] For 200 years has the Gospel there been preached, and to every individual has the truth been fairly offered. An immense amount of ministerial and other labor has there been expended. Extensive revivals of religion have been enjoyed; and there the missionary enterprise has arisen, and with what result? A few years since the estimated population was 2,800,000, and the professed disciples of Christ connected with all the evangelical religious denominations were but 411,000, it being but about one-seventh part of the people. And there are many portions of these very States where the Gospel has been preached with more or less fidelity for, perhaps, half a century, and not one-twelfth part of the population are either professors of religion or habitual attendants on public worship. If such be the fact in the most favored portions of Christendom, are we not constrained to think that the preaching of the Gospel is designed to be merely *a witness* to the nations; gathering some, yea mul-

[1] Lord's Journal, vol. vi, p. 665.

titudes into the fold of Jesus, but not savingly reaching the masses? Has not the Lord, in generations past, been gathering from amid the nations solely an *elect* people? And have we any reason to suppose that it will be different in the years to come preceding the predicted end? Was not the solemn assurance of the Saviour meant for the whole period of this dispensation; "Many are called, but few are chosen?" (Matt. 22:14.) And will it not always be true, until the revelation of the Son of man, that the body of the true disciples is "a little flock?" Is the world actually becoming better? Is it, year by year, assuming more and more the character of the anticipated and predicted season of righteousness and blessedness? Is the age in which we live a purer age than those which have gone before it? Is iniquity less daring? Is infidelity less defiant? Is corruption among men and in government less manifest? Is it so in our own land? Is it so anywhere on the face of the earth? It surely is not difficult for any one to answer these questions in the negative, who looks abroad upon the world.

God, in His providence, is indeed, in these latter days, opening up the way, and, in some instances, in a remarkable manner, for the preaching of the Gospel to benighted nations; but have we not reason to believe, from the history of the past, and from the existing state of things, that this is that the Lord may gather unto himself His own elect? Is it not that the Gospel may be preached "for a witness," in anticipation of the hastening on of the period when the times of the Gentiles will be fulfilled, and the end of this present dispensation shall have come? (Matt. 24:14.) We sometimes try to persuade ourselves that the Gospel is making decided progress, outstripping error, and superstition, and sin, giving promise of its speedy and complete conquest. But is it really so? we again inquire. Will facts warrant this conclusion? Take the last fifty years of our world's history; years during which far more has been done to spread evangelical truth, perhaps, than during any other half century since apostolic days, and has the progress of truth and righteousness outstripped the progress of error and iniquity? Has the Church of Christ actually gained upon the increasing population of our earth? The Church as well as the world has been in an unsettled condition from the very time of Christ's ascension to this hour; and there is no more prospect now that Christianity will settle all these things, by its enlightening and suasive influence, than there was 1800 years ago. Not a solitary kingdom of earth has as yet been recovered from the dominion of the god of this world.[1]

But may we not hope that the Lord is now preparing the way for richer displays of His power and mercy to the world? May we not hope that far greater efficiency will attend the efforts to spread the Gospel, and that thus religion will, ere long, outstrip the progress of iniquity and error,

[1] Duffield.

and, finally supplanting them, introduce the millennium, characterized by universal holiness?

Neither the experience of eighteen hundred years, nor, as we believe, the Scriptures, warrant the anticipation, for, if we read the word of God aright, this wicked world will increase in wickedness. The god of this world will put forth more and more decided effort, and manifest more and more positive influence for evil, as the end approaches (Rev. 12:12); that end which will result in his discomfiture, as he will be bound a thousand years; and when the Lord shall come to terminate sin by the destruction of Antichrist and all His enemies, and to establish His kingdom of peace and righteousness on earth.

We will open the word of God, to see if its teachings corroborate the suggestions of Providence, and to learn whether the second personal coming of Christ will be to introduce the millennium, or to close it. We now consider,

II. *The lessons of Scripture.*

Some of the objects of Christ's coming, as stated in the word of God, would seem to furnish an answer to the question. The establishment of the throne here on earth, on which Christ Jesus is to sit, has been argued, and if the reasoning to show that it must be a literal kingdom was sound, then does it follow that His coming is pre-millennial; for that kingdom is to be established at the time of the restoration of Israel. And that kingdom is the millennium.

We have now before us two facts, which no one

doubts. *First*, that of the personal appearance of Christ, and his actual visible return to our earth, at some time, preceded by the signs of His coming; and, *second*, that of a season of unprecedented glory to the Church. Now this latter day glory for the Church is the time to which patriarchs, prophets, disciples, apostles, martyrs, and godly men in every age, have looked forward with the deepest interest; and in describing it, holy seers have indulged in their loftiest strains, their most enraptured and glowing descriptions. And, surely, if that dispensation of righteousness, and peace, and power, and grace, and blessedness, were immediately to precede the advent of Christ, have we not reason to believe it would have been mentioned as the most prominent and noticeable sign or indication of His coming? Could it have been omitted in the enumeration? But what is the fact? No allusion whatever is made to it as a sign of His advent; and the legitimate inference, the only way, indeed, in which we may account for the omission, is that the coming of Christ in the clouds of heaven is to be before and not after the millennium. He is to *receive* a kingdom, and to *return*, that He *may establish* it. We here may propound the inquiry: If the return of the "nobleman" is not to be until after the millennium, and at the closing up of all terrestrial things, as many in these days affirm—then what becomes of the "kingdom" he had gone to receive, and which on his return he is to bring with him, or to establish, as the statement of Jesus most plainly implies? At the period referred to, "Christ is to *deliver up* the kingdom unto the Father." What, then, becomes of the kingdom He has gone to receive, we again inquire? It is not a spiritual kingdom in the hearts of the regenerate; for that is already set up, even during the absence of the Redeemer. To secure this He left His disciples, that He might send the "Comforter," the "Holy Ghost." We leave the question for solution with those who deny the pre-millennial advent of our blessed Lord.

It is maintained that the Scriptures clearly reveal the fact, that, instead of a gradual improvement in the moral condition of our world, to be consummated by the millennium before the coming of Christ, the same condition of evil for the world and of tribulation for the Church, as in days past, will be continued until the ending of the present dispensation, and the opening of another of great glory, by the appearance of the Son of man. Intimations of this truth are clearly given in the Old Testament Scriptures. But we may confine our examination, just now, to the New. Read carefully the 24th chapter of the Gospel by Matthew. It is the reply of Jesus to the anxious inquiry of His disciples, in reference to the destruction of Jerusalem and His anticipated second advent. "Tell us," said they, "when shall these things be, and what shall be the sign of Thy coming, and of the end of the world?" By the *end of the world* is not meant the destruction of the globe, or the physical, material world. It is important here to note, and we shall have occasion frequently to refer to it, that there are two Greek words, each of which is translated in our version by "world," and yet having very different meanings. The one, "kosmos" (an order or arrangement), has respect to the physical earth, the globe on which we live; the other, "aion," means age, or period, or dispensation. This latter is the word used by the disciples: "What shall be the sign of Thy coming, and the end of the *world*," the end of the "aion," the age, or period, or era, the present, the existing state of things? In the answer of the Saviour, reference is had to both inquiries, or that which has respect to the destruction of the holy city, and that which has respect to the end of the world, or the present age or period. All commentators agree in this. Now read the answer of Jesus, and do it with the remembrance that, as some think, there is in store a thousand years of peace and blessedness before the coming of Christ, and see what confirmation the thought receives. I use the words of another:[1] "It begins with the ruin of Jerusalem, and ends with the second coming. The whole of it is a picture of storm and gloom. It is written, all over, with lamentation, and mourning, and woe. The time which it describes is one of evil throughout; a time of sin—a time of calamity. No gleam of sunshine, no interval of calm relieves the heavy scene in any part, still less towards the

[1] "Proofs of Pre-Millennialism."

close of the era here defined. Clouds thicken and darkness deepens, as the ages roll away. . . . . Jesus gives many minute and palpable signs of His coming; yet they are all dark and fearful. Wars, famines, earthquakes, pestilences, tribulation, persecutions, martyrdom; . . . but no days of prosperous gladness for a weary earth and a harassed Church, as the forerunners of His advent. Not a word respecting a whole millennium of blessedness before His coming, which would, beyond all question, be the brightest and most vivid sign—a sign which could occur but once—a sign beyond the possibility of mistake. Is it conceivable that He could have failed to mention this as one of the signs, if it were really to occur *before* His advent? . . . . And how, moreover, could the evils mentioned *be signs* of *His coming*, if they were all to pass utterly away, and be forgotten for a thousand years? . . . Thus, according to the Lord's own words, the period or era, from the day He uttered the prediction concerning it up to His second coming, was to be a period of evil, not of good; of darkness, not of light, throughout."

In the parallel passage, in St. Luke, we find the significant statement: "Jerusalem shall be trodden down of the Gentiles until the time of the Gentiles shall be fulfilled, *then* shall they see the Son of man coming in a cloud, with power and great glory." (21: 24.) The period of the treading down of the Gentiles, as has already been shown,[1] is the

[1] Chapter 3.

period of Gentile supremacy, the period of Jewish degradation and dispersion. This period being accomplished—the Gospel of the kingdom being preached to every nation "for a witness"—an elect people gathered out from among them—"*then* shall they see the Son of man coming in a cloud with power and great glory." The present condition of things is, then, to continue until brought to an end by the Lord's coming. Is not such the positive prediction; and can it be fulfilled, if the existing degradation and the wide dispersion of the Jews are to end, and be exchanged for glory and restoration, a thousand years before the Redeemer shall come? Does it not appear that the statement of Jesus Himself settles this important question? I confess I know not how to escape the conclusion, that we must look for the Saviour's glorious appearing *before* the world will enjoy the millennium promised.

The same truth is taught in several of the parables. By that of the *Tares and the Wheat.* (Matt. 13.) We are informed that a characteristic of the present state of things is that the false and the true, the evil and the good, are inseparably intermingled. Are they always thus to continue? If the parable have meaning, they are thus to continue until the "*harvest.*" Will no thousand years of righteousness intervene to change this condition of things? No! verily; for thus is it to be *until* "the Son of man shall send forth His angels, and *they* shall gather out of His kingdom all things that offend, and them that do iniquity, and shall cast them into a furnace of fire; there shall be wailing and gnashing of teeth. *Then* shall the righteous shine forth as the sun in the kingdom of their Father." (13:41, 42.) Here we are instructed that things are to continue, without amelioration of evil, as they are, until the Son of man shall come to destroy the evil, and to glorify and to bless His Church. This is to be at the time of the *harvest*, and the harvest is to be the *end of the world*—the end of the "*aion*," age, dispensation, period.

The parable of the "*Net*" gathering every kind, the evil and the good, teaches the same truth precisely. (Matt. 13:47.) The "end of the world," in this parable, is in the original the same as that of the last; "aion," this present period.

It is worthy of special notice, that nowhere in the Scriptures is the world's wide-spread wickedness said to be terminated by the arrival of the millennial age; but in numerous passages in the parables and elsewhere is that wickedness said to be judged, avenged, and swept away by the coming of the Son of man.

In his first Epistle to the Thessalonians, St. Paul makes frequent mention of the coming of the Lord Jesus. He speaks of them as "waiting for the *Son of God from Heaven*, whom He *raised from the dead*." "What is our hope, or joy, or crown of rejoicing? Are not even ye in the presence of our Lord Jesus Christ at his coming?" (2:19.) "To the end he may stablish your hearts unblamable in holiness, before God even our Father, at the coming of our Lord Jesus Christ, with all His saints."

. . . . "For the Lord himself shall descend from heaven with a shout; . . . . and the dead in Christ shall rise first; . . . . for yourselves know perfectly that the day of the Lord so cometh as a thief in the night." From these representations, or in some other way; (it may have been, as some suppose from the context, from a forged letter,) the Thessalonians had been led to think this predicted second coming of the Saviour was immediately at hand. This impression the Apostle wishes to correct. And how does he do it? Is it by stating that they had misunderstood his words, and that they were not to expect the coming of Christ? Is it by instructing them that this coming was figurative, and to be spiritually understood? Is it by informing them that a Millennium of prosperity and joy was to intervene? Read his significant words, and judge; "You who are troubled rest with us, when the Lord Jesus shall be revealed from heaven with His mighty angels; *in flaming fire taking vengeance* on them that know not God and that obey not the Gospel of our Lord Jesus Christ; who shall be punished with everlasting destruction from the presence of the Lord and from the glory of His power; when He shall come to be glorified in His saints, and to be admired in all them that believe in that day. . . . . Now we beseech you, brethren, by the coming of our Lord Jesus Christ, and by our gathering together unto Him, that ye be not soon shaken in mind, ... as that the day of Christ is *at hand.*" He would have them understand that, before that should occur, a certain event must take place, and which they were overlooking. Was this the glorious Millennium? Hear the response of the Apostle: "Let no man deceive you by any means; for that day shall not come except *there come a falling away first*, and that man of sin be revealed, the son of perdition." He then states that this mystery of iniquity was even then beginning to work, but should be restrained for a season, in its full development into the last Antichrist. But when this restraining influence should be taken out of the way, "*then shall that wicked be revealed*, whom the Lord shall *consume with the spirit of His mouth, and shall destroy with the brightness of His coming*." The same great, formidable power of iniquity—the man of sin—the Antichrist, is symbolized by the little horn on the head of the beast, in Daniel's vision, who should "speak great words against the Most High, and should wear out the saints of the Most High." (Dan. 7 : 25.) He is to exist for a season, and then, declares the inspired prophet; "The judgment shall sit, and they shall take away his dominion, to consume and to destroy it unto the end." And this is to be done by one "like unto the Son of man coming in the clouds of heaven." By the *mystery of iniquity*, which was beginning to work in the days of St. Paul, we believe to be meant the Papal apostacy, then in its embryo existence, which increased in subsequent ages, and became the formidable, gigantic antagonist of pure religion, although itself wearing the garb of Christianity; and which shall culminate, as the period of the second advent shall approach, in the "man of sin," *the Antichrist, who is to be consumed by the Spirit of the Redeemer's mouth, and destroyed by the brightness of His coming.* Some seem really to expect that this mighty system of evil—this grand hierarchy of Satanic origin—is to waste away under the gradual extension of the Gospel; and that even this "man of sin" may be, at least partially, "consumed" by the *truth!* A popular commentator on the words, "whom the Lord shall consume with the spirit of His mouth, and shall destroy with the brightness of His coming," says; "The meaning may be, that one of the grand agencies for destroying this antichristian power, is the *truth* spoken or revealed by the Saviour; that is, His pure Gospel. . . . . It cannot be denied, however, that the most obvious interpretation is that which refers both clauses in the sentence to the same period,—that of the second coming. Still, it is not improper to suppose that it may be implied that his power may be weakened and diminished by the influence of the Gospel, though it may not be wholly destroyed until the coming of the Saviour. . . . The words, 'by the brightness of His coming,' would naturally harmonize with the idea that there would be a somewhat gradual process, under the operation of *truth*, toward the destruction of the man of sin; but that the complete annihilation of his power would be by some more manifest exhibition of the personal glory of the Saviour." Now, when is this "exhibition" to be made? It is answered, "brightness" means an appearing, and refers to the manifestation of the Saviour when He "*shall come to judge the world.*" And when shall this be? Not until the Millennium shall have passed! Hence is this "man of sin" the great opposer of the Gospel—the Antichrist—he who "shall speak great words against the Most High, and shall wear out the saints of the Most High;" to exist in and to continue through the Millennium, although he may possibly be somewhat softened in the malignity of his character by the previous influence of the truth—waiting his "destruction" by some signal visitation, at what is supposed will be the judgment at the end of this world—the end of all that pertains to our earth! Can such possibly be the case? Is the existence of such a power, during millennial blessedness, at all consistent with the scriptural representation of that period? By this "man of sin," however, it is thought by some, is meant "the Pope of Rome; not a single Pope, but the succession." *This* system, then, with the Popedom continued, is to remain (under a form, it may be, somewhat modified by the gradual progress of Gospel truth, before the Millennium) during these thousand years of blessedness, to be overtaken and destroyed by the judgment of the Lord at the last day. We cannot so read and so understand the Scripture record.

One thing is very clearly revealed, which is, that this gigantic system will continue (and so far as we can find from the word of God, not with less, but with increased opposition to the Gospel,) until the coming of the Son of man. And if we cannot suppose that its existence can be compatible with the predicted condition of things during the thousand years, then must the coming of our Lord be before the Millennium. It is important to note that it was a literal and personal coming for which the Thessalonian Christians were looking. There can be no doubt of this. The language is too plain to permit a question of it. It was a literal personal coming, which the Apostle says would not occur until a certain event should transpire. It was a literal personal coming which is spoken of in every passage, no less than twelve in number, in these two epistles. It was a literal personal coming to which the whole of the Apostle's argument refers. The reign of this apostate power is then to be during the whole period of the "nobleman's" absence, and only to end when he shall "return." Can there be a Millennium before the advent of the Son of man?

St. Peter, in his second epistle (3 : 1–4), would stir up the minds of his readers to the remembrance of important truths, which he had delivered unto them; on one of which he seems to lay peculiar stress, "Knowing this first, that there shall come, in the last days, scoffers, walking after their own lusts, and saying, Where is the promise of His coming? For since the fathers fell asleep all things continue as they were from the beginning of the creation?" It would appear that these scoffers are prompted to the inquiry by an awakened interest on the subject of Christ's second advent; and they are led, with scornful sarcasm, and in expectation of refuting these anticipations of the glorious "epiphany," and of putting those who believe it to shame, to declare the promise of His coming to be a lie, inasmuch as all things have continued without change, in this respect, from the beginning of the creation. "Where is the promise of His coming?" is their taunting inquiry.

The inspired penman comforts the minds of his readers by showing the fallacy of their reasoning, as he exposes their wilful ignorance, and by referring to the fact that "with the Lord a thousand years are as one day." He then gives a reason why the coming of the Son of man was somewhat delayed. It is because of His long-suffering patience towards the wicked, even towards such impious scoffers as these. "The Lord is not slack concerning His promise [this promise of His coming], as some men count slackness; but is long-suffering to us ward, not willing that any should perish, but that all should come to repentance." Then with emphatic assurance he says, "But the day of the Lord *will come* as a thief in the night; in the which the heavens shall pass away with a great noise, and the elements shall melt with fervent heat." Now, these scoffers, we are told, will be found in the "last days," and will continue to be found, until startled from their impious apathy by the occurrence of the very fact they had so sneeringly ridiculed. Where, we now inquire, is there room for a thousand years of millennial blessedness? Could the writer have had a conjecture, or deemed it possible, that such a period should intervene between the time of these scoffing skeptics and the fulfilment of the "promise?" And if the inspired man of God had no such thought, may we venture to say it is verily so?

To only one more of many passages we may direct attention. "As it was in the days of Noah, so shall it be also in the days of the Son of man. They did eat, they drank, they married wives, they were given in marriage, until the day that Noah entered into the ark, and the flood came and destroyed them all. Likewise, also, as it was in the days of Lot; they did eat, they drank, they bought, they sold, they planted, they builded. But the same day that Lot went out of Sodom, it rained fire and brimstone from heaven, and destroyed them all: *even thus shall it be in the day when the Son of man is revealed.*" (Luke 17:26–30; Matt. 24:37, 38, 39.) Now, this coming or revelation of the Son of man must be either, 1. A *spiritual* coming at the Millennium; or, 2. A coming in judgment at the closing up of the drama of our earth's history (Rev. 20); or, 3. A *providential* coming in judgment upon the Jewish people; or, 4. A *veritable personal coming*, at the end of the present dispensation, and before the Millennium. Is it 1, *a spiritual* coming? We answer in the negative, for two reasons. *First*, the word rendered "coming," (Matt. 24,) will not admit of such an interpretation. It is "*parousia*," which means a personal appearance. Robinson renders it, "the being or becoming present, presence or coming, advent;" and Donnegan, "an arrival." *Secondly.* On the principle of those who consider the coming of the Son of man at the Millennium to be a spiritual coming, to reign in the hearts of His people, no such scene as that here described can possibly exist at the time. The Millennium is to be brought about, we are told, by agencies now employed, and the gradual, moral improvement of the world, resulting in a season of universal righteousness. If so, can there be at the time predicted a state of society like that of the "days of Noah" and "the days of Lot," as here described—a season of prevalent wickedness, and worldliness, and sensuality? But may not the coming be, 2, the Lord's coming in Judgment? That coming which is described, at the close of the 20th chapter of the Revelation, a coming to wind up the affairs of time and of our world? We think not. His coming then will, indeed, be a "parousia," a personal advent. But under what circumstances will His appearing be? It will be amid scenes of dreadful commotion. The confederate hosts of the enemies of God, collected by Satan, now loose for a season, will be gathered together for *battle*, and not for peaceful carnal indulgence, and in perfect indifference, as were the antediluvians and the inhabitants of Sodom. Surely reference cannot be had to that season of fearful interest, when the foes of Jehovah being destroyed and Satan cast into the burning lake, the Judge shall be seen upon His great white throne, to pass sentence on the wicked dead now raised. May it not be, 3dly, a *providential* coming, referring especially to the Jewish nation, as the destruction of the city and the dispersion of the people? We think not. And that, first, because the context seems most clearly to point to some other and more startling important event. That visitation of affliction, which continues through the whole period of their dispersion—"the times of the Gentiles,"—up to the very end of the dispensation, is spoken of by the Saviour, and He then declares that, immediately *after* the tribulation of those days, there should be various phenomena, well calculated to arrest attention, and which should be as "signs" of the eve of some grand exhibition of glory and of power. "And then shall appear the sign of the Son of man in heaven. . . . . And they shall *see the Son of man coming in the clouds of heaven with power and great glory*, and He shall send His angels with a great sound of a trumpet, and they shall gather together His elect . . . . from one end of heaven to the other;" and at that time "shall *all the tribes* of the earth mourn." This assuredly looks to some other scene than that witnessed when the providence of God visited Jerusalem and the Jewish people with judgments. But, secondly, the coming is, we have seen, a "parousia," a personal appearance, which was not the case when Jerusalem was destroyed. Thus it was not a providential coming of which the Redeemer spoke these emphatic words. Are we not absolutely shut up to the conclusion, 4th, That nothing less is meant, than, that when Christ shall come, in person, at the end of this present order of things, the social condition of the world, and the state of heedless indifference, will be as they were in the days of Noah and of Lot? and if so, must not that promised "parousia," or coming, be before the Millennium? Such a state of things—such indifference and prevailing worldliness, and general wickedness, could not exist on any other supposition but that Christ will come to *introduce*, by his judgments on the wicked, the season of millennial blessedness. As "the flood came and took away" that wicked generation, and as it "rained fire and brimstone from heaven on the guilty inhabitants of Sodom, and destroyed them all, even thus shall it be when the Son of man is revealed." It will be a fearful scene to the ungodly; but one of rejoicing to the children of God, who shall be waiting for His coming.

These references to the unerring word of truth are sufficient to show what we believe to be the uniform teaching of the Scriptures on this grand subject, THE PRE-MILLENNIAL ADVENT OF THE SON OF MAN, THE NOBLEMAN WHO HAS GONE INTO A FAR COUNTRY TO RECEIVE FOR HIMSELF A KINGDOM, AND TO RETURN.

CHAPTER VI.

MILLENARIANISM NOT A NOVELTY—DESTRUCTION OF THE UNGODLY NATIONS.

DOCTRINE OF PRE-MILLENNIAL ADVENT NO NOVELTY—VIEWS OF THE EARLY CHURCH—OF SUBSEQUENT AGES—AT THE REFORMATION—WHITBY'S "NEW HYPOTHESIS"—THE DOCTRINE GROWING IN FAVOR—PROFESSOR SHEDD REFUTED—CHRIST WILL COME FOR JUDGMENT ON THE NATIONS.

We have not followed cunningly devised fables.—2 PET. 1:16. *When the Lord Jesus shall be revealed from heaven . . . . in flaming fire, taking vengeance on them that know not God.*—2 THESS. 1:7, 8.

THE statement of the Apostle, in his Second Epistle to the Thessalonians, is a dark and painful one. But we are not left without relief. That to which reference is had is not to be a scene of exclusive judgment—for "He shall come to be glorified in His saints, and admired in all them that believe." This is not a cunningly devised fable. It may be proper just here to meet an objection which some may make, or to soften and remove a prejudice which some may have, which is based on the supposition that this doctrine of the personal coming of the Son of man before the Millennium, and the interesting facts which are associated with it, are the crude fancies of these latter days; that they are the doctrines of modern times; unknown to or rejected by the Church in the days of the Apostles and in subsequent centuries.

This is, undoubtedly, an age of novelties. It is an age of wonderful discoveries, and of remarkable inventions. And as truly is it an age of strange delusions and of vain speculations. And some may, some indeed do, consider these views as entertained by the literalists (so called) or the Pre-millennialists, or Millenarians, as crudities whose very *novelty* should condemn them, or, at least, cast upon them a deep shade of suspicion. Are they not to be classed with the unauthorized speculations of Millerism, or with the wild extravagancies of Mormonism, or the delusions of Spiritualism? Whether they deserve to be thus classed and condemned or not, it becomes us to ascertain, as, otherwise, we may, without investigation, possibly be rejecting as false what God has revealed as eternal truth. One thing is very certain, that they are not to be rejected and disbelieved, nor looked upon with suspicion, because of their novelty or supposed first suggestion, in this age of speculation; or because they have not been received and cherished by the orthodox church, in apostolic and subsequent ages. No fact is better established than that these doctrines were held by the Jews previous to and at the advent of Christ. It was a belief derived obviously from the revelations of their Old Testament Scriptures. So they read their own prophets. That they were the teachings of the Saviour and His Apostles, has been abundantly shown in the preceding pages. And that they were the received doctrines of their immediate successors, and of the whole Church, until the beginning of the third century, is susceptible of satisfactory proof. At that time, Origen introduced his allegorical mode of interpreting the Scriptures, in place of the literal, which had previously received the sanction of the fathers of the Church. This was followed by the increasing development of the "mystery of iniquity," which, at the opening of the fifth century and onward, was found to be materially modifying, changing, and perverting the usages, and corrupting the doctrines of the primitive Church. It soon controlled almost universally the belief and practice of nominal Christendom. The millenarianism of the early Church, and with it the Apocalypse itself, was repudiated and rejected as an article of faith. Nor was this without a reason. The fearful judgments threatened against this growing iniquity, and to be inflicted at the second coming of our Lord, made the Papacy the more ready to deny the important doctrine. And, moreover, the coming of Christ to establish His kingdom and personally to reign on earth, being found to conflict with the usurped vice-gerency of him who declared himself the Supreme Head of the Church and the Vicar of Christ; and the doctrine interfering materially, in other respects, with the interests of this apostate hierarchy, the whole subject was ignored; and as a prominent *Papal* historian[1] declares, "rejected everywhere, and derided by the learned with hisses and laughter." Thus the doctrine passed from the accredited creed of the Church.

Bishop Newton, whose work on the prophetic Scriptures has given him an imperishable reputation, says, "Wherever the influence and authority of the Church of Rome hath extended, she hath, by all means, endeavored to discredit this doctrine, and indeed not without sufficient reason—this kingdom of Christ being founded on the ruins of the kingdom of Antichrist. No wonder, therefore, that this doctrine lay depressed for many ages. But it sprang up again at the Reformation, and will flourish together with the study of the Revelation."

At the Reformation it was revived. The most distinguished of the Reformers were, mainly, premillennial in sentiment. Just emerging from the abominations of Popery, the attention of the early reformers was particularly directed to that special subject, the corruptions of Romanism; and the idea of a thousand years of millennial triumph for the Church having been treated with obloquy for ages, they made very little reference to it. But it is a fact that many, if not all of the important truths which are embraced in the scheme, were almost universally entertained by them and

[1] Baronius.

their early successors.[1] The revival of millenarian doctrines was, however, more especially the work of the English Reformers, as Latimer, Ridley, &c., who were decided and avowed advocates of the belief. The doctrine was held by the immediate successors of the Reformers. A majority of the members of the Westminster Assembly of Divines,[2] at which were drawn up a "Directory of Public Worship," the "Confession of Faith," the "Larger and Shorter Catechisms," of the Presbyterian Church, adopted millenarian views.[3] Thus it continued. The most distinguished divines, the brightest luminaries of the Church and general literature, for generations, so understood the Scriptures. A host of illustrious names might be given. Among them we find those of Bishop Latimer, Bradford, Meade, Usher, Charnock, Milton, Cowper, and Sir Isaac Newton. The name of Sir Isaac Newton, it has been well said, "is sufficient of itself to shield the doctrine from the charge of weakness or fanaticism, or of being supported by insufficient evidence. He gave his powerful mind, for two whole years, to the study of the Prophecies, and has avowed his belief in the pre-millennial advent of Christ."[4]

It is a noteworthy fact, admitting of ample

[1] Duffield. [2] 1643.

[3] Robert Bailie, a member of the Assembly, and himself strongly opposed to the doctrine, says, "Most of the chief divines here . . . are avowed Chiliasts" (Millenarians).

[4] Duffield.

proof, that anti-millenarian views, as at present entertained by many, are themselves but of *recent* date. Dr. Daniel Whitby, who died in 1726, was the first to revive Origen's spiritual interpretation of the prophecies. He wrote a Commentary on the Apocalypse, appending to it a treatise on the Millennium; denying the distinctive features of the ancient millenarian faith, and spiritualizing the restoration of the Jews, the coming of Christ, and the first resurrection. He himself calls his views "*A New Hypothesis;*" thus declaring them to be different from those held by his predecessors. And well has he termed it an *hypothesis*, which, according to Webster's definition, is a system or doctrine founded on theory, or on some principle *not proved.*

The early divines of New England, the Cottons and Mathers, and their contemporaries, knew nothing of such a Millennium as that advocated by this commentator. They were decided and avowed Millenarians. Some, however, prominent in the Church, subsequently adopted his views, and this gradually increased until the prevalent sentiment became adverse to that which was held for ages following the Apostles, and which many of the Reformers and the Church for centuries maintained. But the faith of the early Church, and of the Reformers and their successors, is revived. Many have, within these latter days, and especially within the last thirty or forty years, been led, by careful investigation of the Prophecies, to believe that many of the glorious things spoken of Zion have been lost sight of, by giving to the Scriptures a spiritual and not a literal interpretation. And it is a fact worthy of special attention, that, with but few exceptions, modern students of the prophecies, who have published on the subject, are the avowed, uncompromising advocates of these views. In Scotland and England, Millenarianism has gained an extended prevalence, and the belief is constantly increasing; as it likewise is in our own land. Many high in the several evangelical churches, and of extensive reputation for usefulness and careful investigation, have fully adopted these opinions.

Macaulay, the historian, in his essay on the Jews, remarks, "The Christian believes, as well as the Jew, that at some future period the present order of things will come to an end. Nay, many Christians believe that the Messiah will shortly establish a kingdom on the earth, and reign visibly over all its inhabitants. The number of people who hold it is very much greater than the number of Jews residing in England. Many of those who hold it are distinguished by rank, wealth, and ability. It is preached from the pulpits both of the Scottish and English Churches. Noblemen and members of Parliament have written in defence of it. They expect that before this generation shall pass away, all the kingdoms of the earth will be swallowed up in one divine empire."

That this belief in these things has been held

since the days of the Apostles, might be shown, were it needful, by a reference to historic record.[1] The late Bishop Hopkins says; "The fact is, that the commonly received opinion of a spiritual Millennium, consisting in an universal triumph of the Gospel, and the conversion of all nations for a thousand years, before the coming of Christ, is a novel doctrine, unknown to the Church for the space of six hundred years. We may safely challenge its advocates to produce one distinguished writer in its favor, before the commencement of the eighteenth century."[2]

Because most of us from our childhood have been taught to give a spiritual meaning to these prophecies yet to be fulfilled, the suggestion of a strictly literal interpretation, naturally strikes the mind, at first, as something strangely new; and conflicting, as it is supposed to do, with the re-

[1] Professor Shedd, of the New York Union Theological Seminary, in his "History of Christian Doctrines," having examined the claims of Millenarianism to attention, sums up the results of his investigations with the following statements: "1. Millenarianism was never the *ecumenical faith of the Church, and never entered as an article into any of the creeds.* 2. That Millenarianism has been the *opinion of individuals and parties only*, some of whom have stood in agreement with the Catholic faith, and some in opposition to it." (II, p. 398.) For a *triumphant* refutation of these positions, and for a *correct historical* statement of the doctrine, as held from the days of the Apostles, and for a correction, also, of the false positions of Dr. Hatfield, in his papers on the Messiah's second advent, as published in the "American Presbyterian and Theological Review," April and July, 1864, see Shimeall's "Second Coming of Christ."

[2] Quoted by William Newton.

ceived belief of the Church in all past time, should be rejected as an opinion not worthy of adoption, if, indeed, worthy of serious examination. But so far from this being the case, the doctrine, as we have seen, was held by the Church in its purest and best days; and the charge of novelty lies, with all its weight, against those who give to the prophecies a spiritual and not a literal interpretation.

With all prejudice arising from this source—the novelty of these doctrines—removed, we may, with more probability of reaching the truth, address ourselves to the teaching of the word of God.

If the advent of Christ, spoken of by Paul (2 Thess. 1 : 7–10), be before the Millennium, as the context seems plainly to teach us that it is, then will that second advent be accompanied by *signal judgments upon the enemies of God*, even "them that know not God, and obey not the Gospel of our Lord Jesus Christ;" giving us thus the additional proof that there is to be no universal spread of Christianity—no general conversion of the nations before the personal coming of the Son of man. The parable of the tares and the wheat, already examined, and that of the net, gathering both good and bad, plainly indicate that such is to be the case. "The Son of man shall send forth His angels, and they shall gather out of His kingdom all things that offend, and them which do iniquity, and shall cast them into a furnace of fire." They are to be utterly destroyed. This is to be done at the end of this "aion," world, age, or dispensation.

It is clearly revealed, that at the coming of Christ the world, generally, will be in a state of perfect peace and quietude, as respects any apparent impending judgments, or as respects any apprehensions of evil—as was the case in the days of Noah and of Lot. The evil are to be taken absolutely by surprise, and to be filled with consternation and dismay at the sudden coming of our Lord in judgment upon them. As shown in the preceding discussion, this visitation of judgment must be before the Millennium.

In the twentieth chapter of the Revelation mention is made of the Millennium; the binding of Satan for a thousand years; the resurrection of the saints, and the reign of Christ. In the nineteenth chapter—that is in immediate connection with it—we find these emphatic words, giving a statement of what is to precede the thousand years of blessedness. The representation is symbolical, but the general import is obvious. "And I saw the heaven opened, and behold a white horse, and He that sat upon him was called Faithful and True, and in righteousness He doth *judge* and *make war;* . . . . and He was clothed in a *vesture dipped in blood*, and His name is called the WORD OF GOD. And the armies which were in heaven followed Him upon white horses, clothed in fine linen, white and clean. And out of His mouth goeth a sharp sword, that with it He should *smite the nations;* and He shall rule them with a *rod of iron;* and He treadeth the winepress of the *fierceness and wrath* of Almighty God. And He hath on His vesture and on His thigh a name written, KING OF KINGS AND LORD OF LORDS. . . . And I saw the beast and the kings of the earth, and their armies gathered together to make war against Him that sat on the horse and against His army. And the beast was taken, and with him the false prophet who wrought miracles before him, with which he deceived them that had received the mark of the beast, and them that worshipped his image. These both were cast alive into a lake of fire, burning with brimstone. And the *remnant were slain* with the sword of Him that sat upon the horse." (Vv. 11–20.)

Symbolical as this language is, we repeat there is no mistaking its general meaning. It clearly represents the Son of God coming to execute judgment upon the ungodly, immediately preceding the thousand years of peace. The passage forcibly reminds us of the words of Isaiah, referring to the same eventful period; "Who is this that cometh from Edom, with dyed garments from Bozrah? This that is glorious in His apparel, travelling in the greatness of His strength? I that speak in righteousness, mighty to save! Wherefore art Thou red in Thine apparel and Thy garments like him that treadeth in the winefat? I have trodden the wine-press alone . . . . for I will *tread them in Mine anger and trample them in My fury; and their blood shall be sprinkled upon My garments; and I will stain all my raiment. For the day of vengeance is in Mine heart*, and the year of My redeemed is come; . . . I will *tread down the people* in Mine anger, and make them drunk in My fury." (63:1–6.) This passage is, not unfrequently, very strangely applied to the Lord Jesus Christ, at His first coming to make an atonement for sin. The language will not admit of such an application. He then came to shed His own blood, not to be stained with that of His enemies. Then He came to manifest His loving kindness and tender mercy towards His oppressors, making intercession for them in the very agonies of a cruel death—by them inflicted. Here He treads them down in His anger, and tramples them in His fury. At that time all was peace and love and proffered pardon. Here He has a "*day of vengeance in His heart.*" It is fearful language, and surely is significant, and cannot have been verified when He came the compassionate Redeemer—the predicted "*Lamb* of God." It must anticipate that coming which is to be so startling to the slumbering nations of the earth, when He shall say concerning His enemies, who would not have Him to reign over them, "Bring them forth and slay them before Me."

Hear again the words of the same prophet in the 24th chapter; "Behold the Lord maketh the earth empty, and maketh it waste and turneth it upside down, and scattereth abroad the inhabitants thereof. . . . . And it shall come to pass in that day that the Lord shall punish the hosts of the high ones that are on high, and the kings of the earth upon the earth." And to what day has the prophet reference? He himself responds; "When the Lord of hosts shall reign in Mount Zion and in Jerusalem, and before His ancients gloriously." (v. 23.) "Let the earth hear and all that is therein, . . . for the indignation of the Lord is upon all nations, and His fury upon all their armies. . . . The sword of the Lord is filled with blood. . . . It is the day of the Lord's vengeance, and the year of recompenses for the controversy of Zion." (34:1–8.)

The Scriptures, moreover, clearly reveal the fact that this destruction of the guilty nations will be at the restoration of the Hebrew people,[1] and this, as already stated, will immediately precede the Millennium, and be connected with its introduction. "Therefore fear thou not, O my servant Jacob, saith the Lord; neither be dismayed, O Israel: for, lo, I will save thee from afar, and thy seed from the land of their captivity; and Jacob shall return, and shall be in rest, and in quiet, and none shall make him afraid. For I am with thee, saith the Lord, to save thee: though I make a full end of all nations whither I have scattered thee, yet will I not make a full end of thee." (Jer. 30:10, 11.) "Behold I will make Jerusalem a cup of trembling unto all the people round about. . . . . And in that day will I make Jerusalem a burdensome stone for all people: all that burden themselves with it shall be cut in pieces."

[1] See chap. 6.

(Zech. 12 : 2.) The time when Michael the prince shall stand up for Daniel's people, and cause their scattering to cease, shall be "a time of trouble, such as never was since there was a nation, even to that same time." (Dan. 12 : 1.)

Besides the idolatry, infidelity, impiety, oppression, injustice and general depravation of manners which are mentioned by the prophets as the procuring causes of these exterminating calamities, the cruelties inflicted by the nations upon the *house of Israel* are particularly distinguished. Thus saith the Lord of hosts; "In those days when I shall bring again the captivity of Judah and Jerusalem, I will also gather all nations . . . . and will plead with *them for My people*, and for My heritage Israel, whom *they have scattered* among the nations, and parted My land. . . . . Behold I will raise them out of the place whither ye have sold them, and will return *your recompense upon your* own head." (Joel 3.) This third chapter of the prophecy of Joel is of startling interest in its reference to the judgments to be inflicted on the nations at the last day. A challenge is publicly proclaimed to the enemies of God to gather themselves together and prepare for a deadly conflict. The harvest being ripe, the avenging agents are bidden to thrust in the sickle for the dreadful work of destruction. "The whole visible creation is thrown into the most violent commotion, as if the final dissolution of all things had come." Amid these direful calamities, Jehovah is declared to be the hope and strength of

His people. And they are thus encouraged to confide in His protection. The energetic language of the prophet has surely had nothing to meet it in anything that took place between the captivity and the birth of the lowly babe at Bethlehem. It is to be verified, in its solemn import, at a time yet future. Scott remarks, "Almost all the prophets foretell the same final victory over all the nations, about the time when the Jews shall be restored to their own land; and just before the Millennium, when the kingdoms of this world shall become the kingdoms of our Lord and of His Christ." Events preceding the Millennium are evidently intended—"Although," he says, "the sublime description cannot but lead the reader to think of the end of the world, the day of judgment and the heavenly Jerusalem."

Here as elsewhere, it is clearly revealed that there shall be a mighty combination of the powers of the earth at that time. They consult together to overthrow His cause. They band themselves together to fight against it. It will be such a gathering as earth has never seen. They will "rage and the people imagine a vain thing. The kings of the earth shall set themselves, and the rulers take counsel together against the Lord and against His Anointed. But He that sitteth in the heavens shall laugh. The Lord shall have them in derision. . . . . *Thou shalt break them with a rod of iron. Thou shalt dash them in pieces like a potter's vessel.*" (Ps. 2.)

The heathen shall indeed be given to Christ for

an "inheritance, and the uttermost parts of the earth for a possession." But it will be accompanied or preceded by these exterminating judgments upon the ungodly, anti-christian, infidel, opposing nations of the earth. Those who shall have risen up in avowed hostility against Christ, saying; "This man shall not rule over us," will be visited with fearful calamities. And the rest shall be spared and given to Christ for an inheritance, the subjects of His Kingdom.

Thus are the predicted events of the closing of the present dispensation, to be amidst startling revolutions. The Stone, cut out of the mountain without hands, is to *smite* the image and *destroy* it; and then, we are taught, great voices shall be heard in heaven, saying; "The kingdoms [or the dominion] of this world are become the dominion of our Lord and His Christ, and He shall reign for ever and ever."

Fearful, indeed, are the coming judgments; The words of St. Paul will be fully verified! The Lord will come "in flaming fire, taking vengeance on them that know not God and obey not the Gospel of our Lord Jesus Christ." (2 Thess. 1:8.) This, it is thought by some, will be at the judgment of the "Great Day," at the end of all things. Whereas it will be the commencement of the predicted judgment of the nations—not to be after a thousand years of millennial blessedness, but to introduce them. Great commotions and mighty revolutions are to characterize this eventful period.

How impressive are the utterances of Jeremiah. The prophet was commanded to take a wine cup and make the nations drink. They were all to drink, and after naming them, He sums them all up in these words; "And all the kings of the north, far and near, one with another, and all the kingdoms of the world which are upon the face of the earth [shall drink of them]. . . . And it shall be, if they refuse to take the cup at thine hand to drink, then shalt thou say unto them; Thus saith the Lord of hosts, ye shall certainly drink. . . . . Ye shall not be unpunished; for I will call for a sword upon all the inhabitants of the earth, saith the Lord of hosts." (Jer. 25.)

We may with these assurances of the Word of God, in reference to the judgments to be inflicted upon the guilty nations of the earth, before us, be enabled the better to understand a scene depicted in the 25th chapter of Matthew, and which is generally referred to a very different period, "When the Son of Man shall come in His glory, and all the holy angels with Him, then shall He sit upon the throne of His glory, and before Him shall be gathered all nations, and He shall separate them one from another as a shepherd divideth the sheep from the goats; and He shall set the sheep on His right hand, but the goats on the left." The judgment passed is one of joyous invitation to the blessedness of the Kingdom for the one class; but to the other a sentence of banishment to everlasting fire.

It is usually supposed that this implies a universal, promiscuous resurrection of the dead and a simultaneous judgment of the race at the very end of all earthly things.

An examination of the passage may tend to correct this impression. It is stated that before the Son of Man, now come in His glory, shall be gathered all *nations*. The word "nations" is never used in the Scriptures for *dead*, but for *living* communities. The word in the original always means the population living at the period to which the expression, in which it is employed, refers. The dead are not known as nations. And there is not, moreover, the slightest allusion in the narrative to a resurrection from the dead. Those who are gathered together are there as *nations*, not as *individuals*. The judgment is a judgment of nations, and it has exclusive reference to the treatment which the people of God have received at their hands. This is the ground of condemnation or of acquittal. The treatment which the followers of Christ shall have received is virtually the treatment He Himself shall have received. Those nations which shall have persecuted the Jews, who have been scattered all over the earth, and those which shall have oppressed and persecuted the Church of God, are the goats which the Judge will give to destruction.

A careful examination of the passage will lead to the conviction that it is but one of those predictions of which the Scriptures are full, which speak of signal judgments to be inflicted on the anti-christian nations of the earth at the coming of the Son of Man to introduce the Millennium. Painful indeed is the thought that such direful calamities, in vindication of the honor and truthfulness of God, and for the interests of Zion, must be experienced.

"Go ye into all the world and preach the Gospel unto every creature," was the merciful commission of the Great Head of the Church. "Repentance and remission of sins are to be preached in His name, among all nations." "And ye, saith the Lord, are witnesses of these things." Thus are these glad tidings of mercy to be proclaimed abroad, and salvation, in the name of Christ, to be offered unto all. A fair and full opportunity is to be given to the nations to yield to the righteous dominion of the Prince of Israel, the incarnate Jesus. Many have accepted and many will yet accept the terms of life. And a host will thus be gathered out from among the Gentiles for the praise of God; while yet the large majority, we fear, will continue as they ever have, to reject the proffered mercy. The god of this world or age, will, for a season yet, exult in his dominion. The Gospel will be preached, though disregarded—salvation offered, though rejected. And the time will come, and it seems to be coming on apace, when severest judgments must overtake the ungodly. The Gospel of the Kingdom shall "be preached in all the world for a witness unto all nations, and *then shall the end come.*" Painful as the prospect is—dark and distressing as the scene may be, we may not, to free our hearts from sadness, turn from it, if God has so revealed it. It becomes us to know the truth, and well to ponder it, for our dearest interests and the interests of the Church of God, are intimately interwoven with it.

We may have looked with admiration upon the scene the skilful artist has spread upon the canvas. The foreground of the picture is the representation of ruin, calamity, and woe; with a master's hand, but with dark pencilling, he has spread before us scenes of startling desolation. The lowering cloud surcharged with all the enginery of destruction, hangs its dark, portentous folds over all. There is nothing in this foreground to relieve the eye. It is dark, comfortless, dreary, confused, startling. It is, however, but the foreground of the picture. That dark cloud is tinged, you see, with light, and beyond the scene of desolation shine forth the brightest, most gladsome conceptions of the artist's mind. It is a paridisiac scene of loveliness.

So is it with the inspired limners of the scenes before us. If prophecy reveals these coming calamities, these seasons of startling revolutions, and upheavings of the nations of the earth, there are beyond them all, or associated with them, visions of transcendent glory. For if "the Lord Jesus Christ shall be revealed from heaven, with His mighty angels, taking vengeance on them that know not God," He will also come "to be glorified in His saints, and admired in all them that believe," thus verifying to the Church the glorious things promised to Zion. If He comes to destroy and remove what has opposed His righteous government and left its blight upon the earth, it will be that on the earth, renovated and made pure, He may establish His own ever blessed Kingdom—gather together His ransomed people and banish the arch-enemy of man to the bottomless pit, and introduce a Millennium of unprecedented glory.

CHAPTER VII.

A RENOVATED, NOT A DESTROYED EARTH—THE FIRST RESURRECTION.

DESTRUCTION OF THE EARTH—BAPTISM OF FIRE—TWO SPECIAL OBJECTS CONTEMPLATED—OCCUPANTS OF THE NEW EARTH—TWO RESURRECTIONS—THE FIRST RESURRECTION.

A new earth wherein dwelleth righteousness.—2 PET. 3: 13.
The dead in Christ shall rise first.—1 THESS. 4: 16.

As the Thessalonian Christians had misunderstood the instructions of St. Paul, and were led to think that the advent was immediately at hand, or had already come; so it is evident that, among those to whom St. Peter addressed his epistle, there were some who totally ignored any such event as a second coming of our Lord. St. Paul corrects the error of the Church at Thessalonica in his second epistle; and St. Peter gives an emphatic assurance, that the doctrine was not "a cunningly devised fable," a fiction invented by designing men, but a solemn, indisputable fact. And most evidently is it such; and one which, in the period of its occurrence, and in its immediately antecedent, accompanying and following events, should be carefully and devoutly studied. Much, in reference to these things, is made known in the word of God; while other things, about which an awakened curiosity may propound a variety of questions, are only to be known hereafter; as no solution of the question is given. It is with the facts, as revealed, we have to do; and these are not to be discredited or disregarded, because all that may be asked in reference to them cannot be readily answered. Bearing this in mind, we continue our discussion; and pass to consider,

1. A Renovated Earth.
2. The First Resurrection.

I. A Renovated Earth.

The fact of a kingdom to be established here on earth has been argued; a kingdom of which Christ Jesus is to be the reigning Prince. And we have maintained that this is to be a literal kingdom; one over which the Redeemer, in person, as its visible Head, is to rule; and not solely or exclusively a spiritual dominion in the hearts of believers. But how can this earth be the scene of this glorious government, the place where Christ will personally reign, with his risen saints, over his ransomed Church, in their natural bodies, inasmuch as the Scriptures speak of the "end of the world," and the destruction of this earth by fire? This is the point now to be considered.

It must be borne in mind, as has been stated in the previous discussion, that there are, in the original Greek of the New Testament, two words of very different import, but both rendered, in our translation, by "world." One, "kosmos," means the order and visible arrangement of the earth. The other, "aion," means age, era, dispensation, period, always having respect to time—duration. Now, "end of the world" is a scriptural expression; but it never is found, we believe, in a single instance where the word rendered "world," is that which means the material earth. It is, in every case, that which embraces the idea of time or duration, and expresses a period, or age, &c. (Matt. 13:39, 40; 24:3; 28:20.)

Strong, indeed, and startling is the language used by inspired men to designate the change this material earth is to undergo at the second advent of the Son of man, whenever that advent shall occur, whether before or after the Millennium.[1] By many of those who suppose that the coming of the Son of man in the clouds of hea-

[1] It is maintained by some, that although there will be a renovated earth at the Millennium, the universal conflagration—the sweeping desolation by fire spoken of by the Apostle—will follow and not precede the Millennium. It is thought that there are to be two acts of judgment, two conflagrations, entirely separate and distinct in their order of time, as well as in their extent. So that the "new heavens and earth" predicted by Isaiah 65:17-20, and 66:22-24, the result of the first *partial* visitation of fire, are the renovated "heavens and earth," at and during the millennial period; and that the "new heavens and earth" of 2 Pet. 3:7-13, and Rev. 21:1-5—the result of a second more general conflagration—are post-millennial—a thousand years or more intervening between the two. See this subject argued in Shimeall's "Second Advent of Christ." 204-216.

ven is not to be until the predicted period of a "thousand years" shall have ended, it is thought that He will then come to call the dead of all preceding ages from their graves to judgment; which past, this earth will be annihilated—totally destroyed by fire. By those who maintain that the coming of Christ for judgment, and for the establishment of His kingdom, will be before and to usher in the Millennium, it is believed that there will, at His coming, be a fiery expression of the Lord's indignation against His enemies, and an essential change wrought upon this material world; purifying and making it the fit habitation of a blessed, ransomed race, under the dominion of the visible King of Zion and His glorified Church. If it can be shown that the earth is to be absolutely destroyed by fire—annihilated—put out of existence, or made positively unfit for habitation, at the coming of the Son of man, then, obviously, is the question of His personal reign on earth, during the Millennium and subsequently, forever definitely settled. Such a reign would be an utter impossibility. Hence the importance of learning, if we can, what the expressions mean. The Psalmist declares—and his words are quoted by St. Paul in his Epistle to the Hebrews—"Of old hast thou laid the foundations of the earth, and the heavens are the work of thy hands. They shall perish, but thou shalt endure. Yea all of them shall wax old like a garment. As a vesture shalt thou change them, and they shall be changed." (Ps. 102:25, 26.) St. Peter, alluding to the deluge, says, "The world that then was, being overflowed with water, *perished;* but the heavens and the earth which are now, by the same word, are kept in store, reserved unto fire against the day of judgment and perdition of ungodly men. . . . . The day of the Lord will come as a thief in the night, in the which the heavens will pass away with a great noise, and the elements shall melt with fervent heat, and the earth also and the works that are therein shall be burned up. . . . Looking for and hastening unto the coming of the day of God, wherein the heavens, being on fire, shall be dissolved, and the elements shall melt with fervent heat." (2 Pet. 3.)

Here, if anywhere, are we taught the total extinction and removal of our globe, at the coming of our Lord. The language, we admit, is strong; but is this the import of the record? The Psalmist, quoted by the Apostle, speaks of the *perishing* of the heavens and the earth; but he seems immediately to explain his meaning, as he says, "as a vesture shalt thou *change* them, and they shall be *changed.*" A material *change* shall be wrought, but not destruction. St. Peter says, "The heavens and the earth are kept in store, reserved unto fire. When the elements shall melt with fervent heat, and the earth be burned up." This reads very much like a destruction, such as, absolutely, to unfit it for habitation, if, indeed, it be not its total annihilation. But you note that he alludes to this same world having *perished* when overflowed with water; and he compares the result of the baptism of fire to the effect produced by the flood. He refers, obviously, to a change, and not to an utter destruction; except so far as there was then, and is to be, at the second coming of Christ, a *destruction of the wicked—the perdition of ungodly men*—for which, he states, expressly, "the earth is kept in store, reserved unto fire against the day of judgment." The world perished by the flood, the world of the ungodly. So will the world of the ungodly perish under the inflicted judgments of the Son of man; for he is elsewhere said to be *coming in flaming fire*, taking vengeance, or righteous retribution, on them that know not God. That such is the probable meaning of the strong language of St. Peter, appears, moreover, from the words which immediately follow them. Having spoken of the heavens passing away with a great noise, and the elements melting with fervent heat, and the earth being burned up, he adds —words worthy of our special notice—"Nevertheless we, according to His promise, look for *a new heaven and a new earth, wherein dwelleth righteousness.*" This is a gracious promise. Isaiah declares, "Behold, I create new heavens and a new earth; and the former shall not be remembered. . . . . For as the new heavens and the new earth which I will make, shall remain before me, saith the Lord, so shall your seed and your name remain." (65:17; 66:22.) This was the vision which greeted the eye of St. John: "I saw a new heaven and a new earth; for the first heaven and the first earth were passed away." (Rev. 21:1.)

Now, whatever may be the purposed mission of this fiery element, to be executed at the coming of Christ, it is very clear that it cannot be the *destruction* of the world. Note the words of David: "The world, also, is *stablished* that it *cannot be moved*." (Ps. 93:1.) "Who laid the foundations of the earth that it *shall not be removed forever*." (Ps. 104:5.) Solomon declares, "The earth *abideth forever*." (Ec. 1:4.) Assurances which will surely be verified.

This comparison of the Scriptures seems clearly to show that the effect of the fiery visitation, at the coming of Christ, will not be the absolute destruction of the earth. We have indeed the assurance that the effect to be produced, in one respect at least, will be less destructive than that of the Deluge. The Lord gave to Noah, and thus to us, the promise "*I will not again curse the ground any more for man's sake, neither will I again smite any more every living thing as I have done*." (Gen. 8:21.) This is the declaration of the unerring Jehovah. And *we* may not call in question the veracity of His word, by saying that this earth is to be totally destroyed; or that it is to be made uninhabitable, or that such a conflagration, as that predicted, must be destructive of all life—for He "*will not again smite any more every living thing*." It will indeed be the destruction of the pre-eminently wicked; but multitudes of the race, we have reason to know, will survive the judgments; and these will become the subjects of the Kingdom to be established.

It appears, moreover, much like presumption for any to affirm, as some do, that in such a conflagration as that described, all on the earth must perish; and hence that the doctrine of the establishment of a literal kingdom must be a fallacy. We ask *whose* judgments are these which are to be inflicted? By *whose* power and at *whose* command are these scenes to be enacted? Cannot He who is "wonderful in counsel and excellent in working," secure the accomplishment of His purposes, even though it should require miraculous interposition? Can He not preserve the lives of those He wills to save, even though everything else should be swept from the face of the earth? Shall we thus venture to limit the Almighty? What He has said He certainly will have power and means to execute. If He has said this earth *shall abide forever*, shall *we* say it cannot be? If He declares He will establish His visible Kingdom here, shall *we* say that it is an impossibility?

Those who make these objections seem entirely to ignore the fact that these stupendous effects are to be brought about by supernatural agency. The power and immediate management of the Almighty One will be manifest in them all. The predicted "restitution of all things" will be secured by a series of miracles, we have reason to believe, such as the world has never witnessed. The admission of the fact of a divine agency, and we presume no one will question it, meets every difficulty which we, in our finite understanding, may not be able to clear away, making, what appears to some, an improbability—nay, an impossibility—an absolute certainty, if the Word of God has so declared it.

It is thought by some that the changes which are to be wrought by the agency of fire, will not be effected at one specific time, either at the commencement or at the close of the millennium. It is indeed certain that what is said, at least, of the destruction of the wicked enemies of the Lord by fire, embraces two distinct events, separated by a period of a thousand years; as is manifest by a comparison of 2 Thess. 1 : 8, and Rev. 20 : 9, in each of which passages a fiery judgment is predicted; one at the beginning, the other at the close of the Millennium.

We remark, furthermore, that while the passages which speak of this fearful visitation of fire, are shown, by a comparison of Scriptures, not to mean the real destruction of the earth in the ordinary acceptation of the word; neither does the language used by the sacred penman necessarily imply so extensive an effect as many ascribe to it. The result of an examination by competent expositors, is that it all may be legitimately and properly rendered without producing the impression which a bare reading of our translation makes on the minds of many.[1] "*The heavens*," it is written, "*are to be on fire*." By the "heavens" we are to understand the air, the atmosphere around us, the region

[1] Daniel Lord; Jos. H. Seiss, D.D., &c.; Robinson's Lexicon.

of clouds, &c. Thus is the word frequently used in the Bible, and their "*being on fire*" may simply mean inflamed, made fiery, or, according to Professor Robinson, "tried with fire, purified, inflamed," "and may be considered as having its import, in this place, exhausted by a condition of the atmosphere in which it is heated, filled with fiery, volcanic emissions, and lit up with lightnings." "*They shall pass away* with a great noise." The literal meaning of the verb is "*to pass along by.*" "So that no man *might pass by* that way." (Matt. 8 : 28; Luke 18 : 37.) It indicates motion, and here with its connection, expresses violent commotion of the wind—the rushing by, like a tornado, or whirlwind, or furious blast like that from a volcanic eruption. *The heavens* (air, atmosphere) *are to "be dissolved.*" The word rendered "dissolved" is to *let loose*, to unbind, untie, as the Saviour said of the colt, "Loose (untie) him." (Mark 11 : 2.) "Doth not each one of you loose his ox." (Luke 13 : 15.) It here refers to the letting loose of those influences which now bind the world in quiet; or the giving freedom to agencies or elements which, rushing forth in unrestrained fury, would produce violent commotion; as the projection into the atmosphere of the contents of a burning volcano. The "*elements are to melt with fervent heat.*" This expression occurs in two closely connected verses. (2 Pet. 3 : 10 and 12.) In the first the word rendered "melt" is the same as that used in verse 12, where the *heavens* are spoken of as being "*dissolved*," loosened, unbound. See Luke 3 : 16. In the second the word is somewhat stronger in meaning, "melt or make liquid." But its import may be determined by the parallel expression of verse 10. "*With fervent heat*," is the participle of a verb meaning to be set on fire, inflamed; and the "*elements*" are certain elementary substances of an inflammatory nature, which shall become "*loosed* or *set free*," by being heated and set on fire, as is illustrated in every volcanic eruption. Again, "*the earth and the works that are therein shall be burned up.*" We remark on this passage that "earth" does not necessarily mean the entire globe. In many places it has a restricted and limited application. (Matt. 9 : 31; Mark 6 : 53.) And there is no reason why we may not here limit it to that part or to those portions where signal destruction is to be visited upon the ungodly, and where the Son of Man shall especially manifest His presence. The expression "*burned up*" would seem to imply entire destruction. But although the word in the original often has this meaning, yet it has sometimes that of simply burning without the idea of destruction, or burning up totally. That this partial meaning belongs to it here, appears from what has been said of the analogy between the destruction by the deluge and that which is to be by fire.

This understanding of these several expressions, which seems perfectly legitimate, strengthens the conviction in reference to the extent and nature of the fiery catastrophe, derived from a comparison of Scriptures. That these judgments will be terrific, there can be no doubt, especially to those upon whom the fearful desolations will be visited; and great will be the changes produced. But we find nothing to warrant the belief that the earth is to be made uninhabitable, or to meet with that destruction which some predict.

Reference has been made to volcanic action, and it is supposed that the phenomena of eruptions illustrate the meaning of the language of the Apostle, which we have just considered. And hence it may be worthy of note that there are stored away in the bosom of our very earth, all the elements and materials for the full accomplishment of these predictions without the exercise of miraculous power. All that is needful is for Him who now restrains the action of these internal fires to "loosen," or unbind them, or give them vent, as now to a limited extent He does in volcanic eruptions, and all that is represented by the graphic statement of the Scriptures will be verified. We remember the accounts published of the magnificent but terrific scene in one of the Sandwich Islands, in 1840; and we need but expand the phenomena to have all that the predicted conflagration embraces. No account could do justice to the actual exhibition. "The lava, like an overwhelming flood, sweeping forest, hamlet, plantation, and everything before it, rolled down with resistless energy to the sea, where, leaping a precipice of forty or fifty feet, it poured itself in one vast cataract of fire into the deep below, with loud detonations, fearful hissings, and a thousand unearthly and indescribable sounds. The scene was terribly sublime. Two mighty agencies in collision. Two antagonist and gigantic forces in contact, and producing effects on a scale inconceivably grand! The atmosphere in all directions was filled with ashes, spray and gases, while burning lava as it fell into the water, was shivered into millions of minute particles, and, being thrown back into the air, fell in showers of sand on all the surrounding country. . . . Hills were melted down like wax, by the stream of fire; ravines and deep valleys filled up; and majestic forests disappeared like a feather in the flames. . . . . Night was converted into day on all eastern Hawaii. The light rose and spread like the morning upon the mountains, and its glare was distinctly visible for more than one hundred miles at sea; and at the distance of forty miles, fine print could be read at midnight. . . . . On the leeward side of the stream as it flowed, no one could live within the distance of many miles, on account of the smoke, the impregnation of the atmosphere with pungent and deadly gases, and the fiery showers which were constantly descending and destroying all vegetable life." During this fearful exhibition a class of the people are described as being in the very condition of those before the flood, and the guilty residents of Sodom who were living in perfect indifference while the judgments of Heaven impended. Some indeed "spent most of their time in prayer and religious meetings—some flew in consternation away from the all-devouring element; others wandered idly along its margin, while another class still, coolly pursued their usual avocations, unawed by the burning fury. They ate, drank, bought, sold, planted, builded, apparently indifferent to the roar of consuming forests, the sight of devouring fire, the startling detonations, the hissing of escaping steam, the rending of the earth, the shivering and melting of gigantic rocks, the raging and dashing of fiery waves, the bellowings, the murmurings, the unearthly mutterings coming up from a burning deep. They went carelessly on amid the rain of ashes, sand and fiery scintillations, gazing vacantly on the fearful and ever-varying appearance of the atmosphere, murky, black, livid, blazing, the sudden rising of lofty pillars of flame, the upward curling of ten thousand columns of smoke, and their majestic roll in dense, dingy, lurid or parti-colored clouds. All these moving phenomena were regarded by them as the fall of a shower, or the running of a brook; *while to others they were as the tokens of a burning world, the departing heavens, and* A COMING JUDGE."[1]

Such was the scene exhibited; and well may we suppose that these fires, now restrained—except as we see them in these occasional, partial, and yet fearful manifestations—only wait the mandate

[1] Titus Coan's Letter, Missionary Herald, July, 1841.

of Him who now holds them in abeyance, to come forth to do His work of fiery vengeance on an ungodly world. The thought that they will be called into requisition at the great day of Christ's appearing, receives corroboration from what is deemed by many to be the correct rendering of 2 Pet. 3:7; "The heavens and the earth which *now are stored with fire*," or, as it may be rendered, "treasured up for fire against the day of judgment and perdition of ungodly men."

These are some of the startling scenes before us. The result will be a regenerated—a purified earth. It must be renovated, changed, purified, before it can be the fitting abode of the righteous, under the government of our Emanuel Prince. And such a renovation, and such a change, and such a purification, we believe it will experience. And that appears to be what is meant by the language of the Psalmist and the Apostle. Then will there be a new heaven and a new earth, wherein righteousness shall verily dwell; an earth to be inhabited, we are expressly told, by the saints.

Then, too, will be fulfilled the words of Paul, in the eighth of Romans. A passage which has given commentators trouble, and which is not, we think, to meet with a satisfactory explanation, except in view of the renovation of this material, sin-cursed earth at the coming of Christ. "The earnest expectation of the creature [or creation, this material world], waiteth for the manifestation of the sons of God. . . . . For we know that the whole creation groaneth, and travaileth in pain together until now; . . . because *the creature* [*creation*] *itself also shall be delivered from the bondage of corruption into the glorious liberty of the children of God.*" The period spoken of is the same as that alluded to elsewhere, where it is said, a new and renovated earth shall be given to the people of the Most High. No longer shall it groan under the yoke of corruption. The blight that has been upon it, since for man's sake it was cursed, and which is on it still, will be removed. It is in bondage deep and bitter. It groaneth and travaileth in pain under the heavy pressure laid upon it, and pants to be delivered. The hour of its deliverance will come, and then with man—both redeemed from the curse—will it rejoice for evermore. Yes, there is to be a renovated, purified earth—an earth blessed, perhaps, with more than the beauty and loveliness of Eden—the fit abiding place of the ransomed Church and her glorious Head.

The continuance of the earth is, moreover, apparent from the fact, that it is to be the inheritance of the saints. Frequent are the assurances which the Scriptures give us of this. "The meek shall inherit the earth, . . . and their inheritance shall be forever. . . . Those that wait upon the Lord, they shall inherit the earth. . . . The righteous shall inherit the land, and dwell therein forever. . . . Wait on the Lord and keep His way, and He shall exalt thee to inherit the land: when the wicked are cut off, thou shalt see it." (Ps. 37.)

These promises are thus often repeated in a single psalm, and the assurances of this heirship of the saints is scattered through the prophecies. Some may consider it derogatory to the promised glory of the saints to dwell, and that forever, on this earth, and they may refuse to give it credence. But in the mind of God it is evidently a theme of commanding interest, and the Holy Spirit has recorded, in varied terms, the promise, for the encouragement and consolation of His people, who feel that now they have no inheritance here. Nor would they have while the heavy curse and blight of sin remains. "But they desire a better country, that is, an heavenly," as *this* shall be at the coming of our Lord, when "the kingdom and dominion, and the greatness of the kingdom, *under the whole heaven*, shall be given to the people of the saints of the Most High." (Dan. 7:27.) This very earth is to be the place where Christ shall establish His Kingdom, and where His redeemed shall dwell with Him forever. But it will be, we repeat, a renewed earth. The words of the prophet and those of the apostles will be verified. There *will* be a fearful, fiery visitation to destroy the ungodly and to purify the earth. This is a fact we may not attempt to explain away by any figurative interpretation. Nor may we anticipate the annihilation of our globe. The catastrophe is compared to the flood. That was a literal fact; so will this be a literal occurrence. The *world perished* when deluged by the flood. So will it *perish* when deluged by the flames. The world was *destroyed* by water; so will it be by fire; and yet in neither case annihilated—only changed. This earth will put on a new phase of loveliness at its baptism of fire.

Thus two objects, especially, are to be attained by this startling, yet sublime visitation. One is the destruction of the eminently and persistently ungodly, the avowed enemies of Christ, the confederated, anti-christian, infidel nations existing at the period of Christ's second coming, which is, we are told, to be "the perdition of *ungodly men.*" The other object is to secure "a new heaven and a new earth," for the display of Jehovah's glory, and for the blessedness of the righteous. However some may repudiate the thought that this world—even if regenerated and made a scene of surpassing blessedness—shall ever become the inheritance of God's people and their dwelling-place, yet so the word of the Lord declares that it will be. It is not to be annihilated and blotted from existence, nor would we desire that it ever should be.

Dr. Seiss, speaking of the supposed total destruction of our earth, says, "I have no idea that God will ever unmake His own creation, or that He will blot out the world whose dust His only begotten Son wore upon Him, or that He will destroy the planet which was the birth-place and the tomb of Him in whom He was so well pleased. Redemption cannot involve the destruction of what existed before redemption was necessary, or consistently repeal any existing laws which were ordained before man fell."[1] Dr. Cummings remarks; "The antecedents of our globe are the most brilliant; the historic traditions of our world are the most thrilling; and it seems to me as if it would be an awful catastrophe, if a world, with such antecedents, and such a history, covered with such magnificent footprints, should ever be expunged, or annihilated, or disappear from the orbs and record of the universe. But we know it will not. Its sin will be eliminated, and it will be reconsecrated by the footsteps of its present Lord. . . . This earth has antecedents—historic associations, blessed reminiscences, that will make it the loveliest and the most interesting, and the most beautiful of all the orbs of the sky; and I thank God that I was born, not in Jupiter, nor in Saturn, nor in Mars, nor in some unfallen orb, but in this fallen, but redeemed, and one day to be—regenerated earth."

But who are to possess the earth? Who are to be the occupants of a renovated world? No one who admits the truthfulness of the Bible, for a moment questions the fact of a resurrection both of the righteous and the wicked. But there is a great difference of opinion as to the time when it will, at least in part, take place. Some think—and it is the current opinion of the day—that there is to be no literal resurrection until the Millennium shall have ended; and that then Christ shall come in judgment; call the slumbering dead of all

[1] Parable of the Ten Virgins.

classes, simultaneously, from their graves; assemble them before Him, and, having passed sentence upon each, shall appoint them to their respective and appropriate abodes for eternity, and bid His consuming fire to annihilate the earth. Others cherish a very different view; finding, as they are satisfied they do, reference made to two distinct resurrections, that of the righteous and that of the wicked, separated by an interval of more than a thousand years. This is the specific question now to be subjected to a scriptural test. It is the question of,

II. The First Resurrection.

On opening the word of God, we meet with certain precious promises, which are assuredly to have their fulfilment. They have been already in part referred to, for another purpose, which was to show that the earth was not to be annihilated, because, in its renewed condition, it was to be the perpetual inheritance of the saints. Now we are to inquire, who are these saints by whom the earth is to be inhabited, as either associated with Christ in the judgment or government of the kingdom, or as subjects of it? Thus it is said by the Psalmist, "Evildoers shall be cut off; but those that wait upon the Lord, *they* shall inherit the earth." (37 : 9.) "The *meek* shall inherit the earth, and shall delight themselves in the abundance of peace." "Mine elect shall inherit it, and my servants shall dwell there." (Is. 65 : 9.) This inheritance is to be "forever;" for "the

Lord knoweth the days of the upright, and their inheritance shall be forever." (Ps. 37 : 18.)

This idea of an inheritance for the saints is fully developed in the New Testament Scriptures, where we read of an "inheritance among them that are sanctified." (Acts 20 : 32.) That this inheritance has respect to a state of blessedness, hereafter to be enjoyed, in all the fulness of its possession, when Christ shall come to establish His kingdom here on earth, would appear from what the inspired writers say of it. Thus St. Paul, in his Epistle to the Galatians (3 : 18): "If the inheritance be of the *law*, it is no more of *promise;* but God gave it to Abraham by promise." Now what was the inheritance promised to Abraham? Whatever else it embraced, the possession of the land was assuredly a part. In him were all the nations of the earth to be blessed. Christ was to be his lineal descendant, and in Him was the blessing to be realized. But not only so; but as truly, in the verification of the promise that he should inherit the earth. "The Lord appeared unto Abram, and said, Unto thy seed will I give this land." (Gen. 12 : 7.) "For all the land which thou seest, to thee will I give it, and to thy seed forever. . . . I will give it unto thee." (13 : 15, 17.) The promise was repeated to Isaac (Gen. 26 : 3), and to Jacob (28 : 13, 14). These assurances are yet to be verified.

St. Peter writes; there is "an inheritance incorruptible and undefiled, and that fadeth not away," reserved, indeed, we are told, "in heaven," but to be "*revealed in the last time.*" (I. 1: 4, 5.) And this last time St. Paul declares (2 Thess. 1:7–10) to be "when the Lord Jesus shall be revealed from heaven, . . . taking vengeance on them that know not God; . . . to be glorified in His saints, and to be admired in all them that believe." This inheritance is to be given to *the saints* "who are kept by the power of God, through faith unto salvation." It is, then, a reserved inheritance. And is it not the same which was promised to the Old Testament saints? They were to inherit the earth. And no argument is needful to show that the promise has not yet been fulfilled to them, nor to their seed, nor to any of the saints. In no satisfactory sense can it be said that they now "inherit the earth."

But how are they to inherit it hereafter? The promise surely contemplates their literal existence here on earth as the inheritors of the land. And can it be in any but their *resurrected* state? They are not to inherit the earth and to inhabit it in their spiritual and disembodied natures. No one supposes this. It is to be, if at all, in their glorified humanity. But how can this be? Do the Scriptures warrant any such anticipation?

There is a passage in the First Epistle of St. Paul to the Thessalonians, well calculated to fill the people of God with joyous expectation, and with great present comfort. "If we believe that Jesus died and rose again, even so them also which sleep in Jesus will God bring with Him. For this we say unto you by the word of the Lord, that we which are alive and remain unto the coming of the Lord, shall not prevent [precede or go before] them which are asleep. For the Lord himself shall descend from heaven with a shout, . . . *and the dead in Christ shall rise first;* then we which are alive and remain shall be caught up together with them in the clouds to meet the Lord in the air; and so shall we ever be with the Lord." (4:15–17.) This wonderful scene is to be enacted at the *coming of the Lord.* At that period are the pious dead to be raised from their slumber of months, or years, or centuries, and to be made complete in their humanity, by the reunion of their sanctified spirits with their glorified bodies; while the living saints, beholding the wondrous event, with exultant praise, shall, themselves now glorified, be caught up together with them in the clouds to meet, as they hail with rapturous joy, their coming Lord. But wherefore will these risen dead and these glorified living saints be thus lifted up? Will the Saviour have come to bear them away to some distant place, there eternally to dwell; as He shall call upon the fiery desolation to sweep over this our earth, and blot it forever from existence? If so, what becomes of the promise that the saints shall inherit the earth, and that forever? They pass up to be with Him in the clouds, gathered safely there under His blessed pavilion; while He visits His enemies with "fiery vengeance," sending forth the melting heat to execute its mission of change, of purification and of renovation upon the earth, that it may be prepared for His glorious kingdom, and the joyous abode of His people in millennial blessedness — the promised inheritance of His people. We find in this passage no mention made of the resurrection of the wicked—not the slightest allusion, directly nor by implication, to it. The resurrection is confined to the dead in Christ. "The rest of the dead" live not yet, nor are they called to their final, fearful recompense, as subjects of the resurrection.

St. John, in the twentieth chapter of the Revelation, narrates a vision in which we are all deeply interested, and in which reference is distinctly made to two resurrections. "I saw an angel come down from heaven, having the key of the bottomless pit, and a great chain in his hand. And he laid hold on the dragon, that old serpent, which is the Devil and Satan, and bound him a thousand years, and cast him into the bottomless pit, and shut him up and set a seal upon him, that he should deceive the nations no more till the thousand years should be fulfilled. . . . And I saw thrones, and they sat upon them, and judgment was given unto them. And I saw the souls of them that were beheaded for the witness of Jesus and for the word of God, and which had not worshipped the beast, neither his image, neither had received his mark upon their foreheads or in their hands; and they *lived and reigned* with Christ a thousand years. *But the rest of the dead lived not again* until the thousand years were finished. This is the first resurrection. Blessed and holy is he that hath part in the first resurrection. . . . . Such shall be priests of God and of Christ, and shall reign with Him a thousand years." (1–6.) This statement is in immediate connection with the predicted coming of Christ to destroy His enemies, as recorded in the preceding chapter. It is the second advent of the Redeemer, come to banish Satan from the earth, and to inaugurate the long-desired Millennium. And mention is made of one class of those who shall enjoy the blessedness of that season; they are the subjects of the first resurrection. And who are they, but those who are spoken of by St. Paul in the passage already considered,—the dead in Christ? They, the Apostle says, "will rise first."

Thus, we maintain, there will be a twofold resurrection,—one, that of the righteous, at the *commencement* of the Millennium, which is called the first resurrection; the other, after the expiration of the thousand years, when Satan, having been loosed for a season, and again discomfited, the wicked shall be raised from the dead, and made to stand before the great white throne for judgment, condemnation, and banishment to the "lake of fire." This is the second death. These two resurrections, as they are to be widely separated, so will they greatly differ in the subjects of them. The one class are to live and reign with Christ a thousand years; the other, *who live not again until* the thousand years are finished, rise but to everlasting misery. The words of the Revelation seem to be very explicit; while yet what appears to be their obvious import is denied by some, and a spiritual interpretation is given to them, so as to make the "first resurrection" merely mean a revival of the martyr spirit, or principles, in the days of the Millennium. But how will the context support such an interpretation? They of whom St. John speaks are to *reign* with Christ. They are to be *priests* unto God, and on them the *second death shall have no power*. Can these things be predicated of a martyr spirit or of martyr principles? Can "principles" be made "priests" unto God? And can they be said, with any propriety of language, or any intelligible meaning, to be exempt from the power of the second death, which is the "lake of fire." This word translated "souls," occurs more than one hundred times in the New Testament; but never is it used to denote characteristics, or attributes, or principles. And this passage we cannot reasonably believe to be an exception. But furthermore, if there be an allusion to *any* literal resurrection in the chapter, as all admit there is at the close, then we see not how we can with any consistency escape the conviction that there is to be a literal resurrection of the righteous—a *first* resurrection—separated from that of the wicked by an interval of a thousand years. The expression, "the *rest* of the dead lived not again until the thousand years were fulfilled," most plainly intimates that *some* of the dead did live before that time. The conclusion is attempted to be evaded, or at least the argument in favor of a literal resurrection weakened by the supposition that the expression, "rest of the dead," does not refer to the wicked in distinction from the righteous of a first literal resurrection. "The phrase," we are told, "most naturally refers to the *same general class* which was before mentioned, *the pious dead.* The meaning is, that the martyrs would be honored as if they were raised up and the others not; that is, that special respect will be shown to their principles, their memory, and their character. In other words, that special honor would be shown to a *spirit of eminent piety*, during that period, above the *common* and *ordinary* piety which has been manifested in the Church."

"The rest of the dead" are not to live again until the thousand years be finished. And so declares the *commentator* in another connection, where, in explanation of the preceding verse, he speaks of the honor to be conferred upon those possessing this revived "martyr spirit." "This," it is said, "would not occur in respect to the rest of the dead—even the pious dead, for *their* honors and rewards would *be reserved* for the great day when *all* the dead should be judged according to their deeds." But in apparent contradiction to this, he affirms; "The rest of the dead—the pious dead—*would indeed be raised up* and rewarded, but they would occupy, comparatively, humble places. As if they did not partake in the exalted triumphs when the world should be subdued to the Saviour." Now, if by "the rest of the dead" we are to understand a spirit of less exalted piety which is *to live* after the thousand years, then, as a consequence, there will be, after the Millennium, a lowering down of the standard of pre-eminent, exalted piety which shall have characterized that period, by the intermixture of a piety more *common* and *ordinary* which is then *to live.* Are we indeed to be driven by a proper understanding of the passage to such a conclusion?

Much stress of opposition, however, is laid by some to the doctrine of a literal resurrection, on the fact that St. John uses the word "souls," instead of "bodies," when speaking of those whom he saw, "to live and reign with Christ." "I saw the *souls*, and they lived." The language, however, is in strict conformity with the Scripture usage, by which the word *soul* is very frequently put for the person—body and soul—sometimes for the body alone. "Let my soul live and it shall praise Thee." (Ps. 119:175.) "They smote all the souls that were therein with the edge of the sword." (Josh. 11:11.) "And the same day there were added unto them about three thousand souls." (Acts 2:41.) "And we were, in all, in the ship two hundred and threescore and sixteen souls." (Acts 27:37.) "Jacob and all his kindred, threescore and fifteen souls." (Acts 7:14.) "God will redeem my soul from the power of the grave." (Ps. 49:15.) Thus is it that the word "soul" is often used for the person or animated body; and hence there is not, from this consideration, the shadow of a foundation for an objection to a literal resurrection of the saints at the coming of Christ in millennial glory. St. John saw the *persons* of those whom he describes. These he saw *sitting* on thrones, and *they* were to live and reign with Christ. Surely he does not speak of the resurrection of a *martyr spirit* or of *martyr principles*, but veritable persons. If what he says of the first resurrection may have a spiritual interpretation, so may all that is said in connection with it; and thus the idea of a thousand years of peace and prosperity may be explained away, as may the resurrection subsequently spoken of, and all that is said of the final destiny of the wicked, at the close of the chapter. If one statement be figurative we see not why all must not be.

Professor Moses Stuart, late of Andover Seminary, a bitter opposer of millenarian views,[1] in general, admits that Rev. 20 clearly teaches a twofold resurrection.[2] And he declares, moreover, that the doctrine of a first resurrection, as taught by St. John, "was not novel to the men of his time." "I have my doubts," he says again, "whether the assertion is correct that the doctrine of the first resurrection is nowhere else (than in Rev. 20) to be found in the Scriptures." Such a concession from such a source is worthy of special note.

There is then, we have reason to believe, to be a first resurrection, or that exclusively *of the pious*

[1] See Hints on Prophecy, and Duffield's Reply.

[2] See Commentary.

dead, to occur a thousand years before the second, or that of "the rest of the dead"—the wicked. It is true that there are passages where the resurrection of both classes is spoken of together, as in that solemn declaration of Christ, "All that are in the graves shall hear His voice and shall come forth; they that have done good to the resurrection of life, and they that have done evil unto the resurrection of damnation." (John 5 : 28, 29.) This is the announcement of a grand principle in the moral government of God—the statement of a positive event to occur. *All* are to be raised from the dead. But when or in what order—how related, as to time—are the two classes to be raised? These questions are not answered by the statement; nor was it designed to refer to anything but the grand fact, that all would, at some time or times, be called from their graves. St. Paul in the fifteenth chapter of his First Epistle to the Corinthians, states that "every man shall rise in his own order," or in his own band or rank, as the word means. "Christ the first fruits; afterward they that are Christ's at His coming." (v. 23.)

Olshausen, a celebrated German commentator, says, "This passage is one of those from which we may undeniably conclude that the New Testament acknowledges and accepts the Jewish doctrine of a twofold resurrection; namely, that of the righteous and a general one." In the fourteenth chapter of Luke is found a parable, in which the Saviour speaks of those who should be "recompensed at the *resurrection of the just*," on which the same writer remarks; "The mention of the resurrection of the just, without any occasion to call it forth, is an evident indication that the distinction made by the Jews between the first and second resurrection—a resurrection of the just as separated and distinguished from that of the ungodly, was acknowledged by our Lord as correct; while other passages show that the apostles themselves had also embraced the same distinction. In the book of Revelation the whole conclusion of the work would be entirely unintelligible without it. The rationalistic expositors were unprejudiced enough to acknowledge that the doctrine of a twofold resurrection was supported by the New Testament. But they employed it to prove that the apostles—and in fact, the Saviour Himself—were entangled in Jewish prejudices, or accommodated themselves to such errors." "The distinction," he remarks, "between the two resurrections, stands in closest union with the whole circle of doctrines respecting the final issue of all things, and, only when we adopt it, do many passages of Scripture acquire their true meaning."

In Matt. 22:24, we find the cavilling Sadducees attempting to confound the Saviour by propounding a question, an answer to which must be, they thought, the refutation of the doctrine of the resurrection. They inquired whose *wife* she would be at the resurrection, who should have been married to seven brothers in succession. The Lord's reply was; "Ye do err not knowing the

Scriptures, nor the power of God. For in the resurrection they neither marry nor are given in marriage." Here would seem to be a denial of the marriage relation, and consequently of the increase of the race after the resurrection alluded to; whereas the *prophet* affirms that the race should be continued, increasing under the reign of the Messiah. (Is. 59 : 21; 65 : 20, 23; Zech. 8 : 5.) Are the words of the Saviour and prophet contradictory? They are so if we reject the doctrine of the first resurrection. "Indeed," remarks Olshausen, "it does not appear how this contradiction is to be reconciled without the supposition of a twofold resurrection." Two things are noticeable here. *First*, those of whose resurrection He speaks, are not to marry nor be given in marriage, but are as the angels of God; like them, it may be, in this respect; while yet, *secondly*, the race is to be propagated. Now we are taught that those who are to share in the first resurrection—the children of the resurrection—are in their glorified bodies to *reign with Christ.* (Rev. 20.) They are not the *special subjects* of His Kingdom. And these are those to whom the Saviour refers. They will not marry. There will be others, not the children of this first resurrection—who shall escape the righteous judgments of Heaven at the coming of the Son of man, who shall be the *subjects* of His government. These will marry and be given in marriage, and thus meet the assurance of the prophet. This interpretation of the passage receives confirmation from the Saviour's words, (v. 31,) "The resurrection of the dead," which is the resurrection out of, or from among the dead, a form of expression frequently found, and which "would be inexplicable if it were not derived from the idea that out of the mass of the dead *some* would rise *first.*"

We refer but to one more passage. St. Paul speaking of his zeal in the cause of Christ, and of his great sacrifices for His sake, and of his vigorous efforts in "pressing toward the mark for the prize of the high calling of God in Christ Jesus," says; "*If by any means I might attain unto the resurrection of the dead.*" (Phil. 3:11.) Two things here arrest our attention; *first*, the earnest desire and the persevering effort of the apostle to *attain* the resurrection of the dead. Must he not have had his mind on some peculiar resurrection? Did he not know—did he not everywhere proclaim—often in the very face of ridicule and persecution, the resurrection of the dead—of *all* the dead? and did he not consequently know that he himself would be raised? He surely had reference to a resurrection distinguishable by special characteristics; one which would be of marked blessedness, and a participancy in which would be a most desirable privilege, and consequently worthy of every effort? *If by any means* he might attain unto it. Can we doubt that it was this first resurrection which so occupied his thoughts, and so greatly enlisted his energies? This appears the more certainly to have been the case, *secondly*, from the fact that here also "the resurrection of the dead" is the resurrection *out of* or *from among* the dead; showing that it was not to a general, promiscuous resurrection he referred. "If I might attain unto the resurrection *from among* the dead." But, it is inquired, may not the apostle simply have reference to the blessedness of the righteous at the resurrection of all, both good and bad? He anticipated, we are told, a marked difference in the condition and treatment of the two classes at the great day of Judgment, when all should stand before the great white Throne? Is not the strong language he used merely that of one vigorously striving after salvation—the portion of the righteous? We think not. The peculiar expression "from among," seems to forbid such a conclusion. And, moreover, he himself assures us; "*I know whom* I have believed, and am persuaded that He is able to keep that which I have committed unto Him against that day." (2 Tim. 1: 12.) It was not then merely a desire and effort after salvation that prompted his strong emphatic words. His soul was already stayed on Christ as he penned the words. To a special, peculiar resurrection he looked, and it was, we think, nothing less than that of which the Revelator speaks—the first resurrection.

Thus the several classes, those that are Christ's and those that are not, will all arise, but at different times. The closing words of the angel-messenger to Daniel, were; "Thou shalt rest and *stand in thy lot at the end of the days.*" And so will all the resurrected saints stand each in his own "lot" or rank. "Blessed and holy is he that hath part in the first resurrection; on such the second death hath no power, but they shall be priests of God and of Christ, and shall reign with Him a thousand years. But the *rest* of the dead *lived* not again until the thousand years were finished." (Rev. 20: 5, 6.)

Thus we have stated an answer in part to the question propounded—who will be with the glorified Redeemer here on earth when He shall have established His Kingdom? They are those who are living at the time, and who shall be in Christ at His coming; and the innumerable hosts of the departed saints of all past generations, from the days of Adam onward to the blessed appearing of the Son of man; all now with bodies like unto the glorified body of the Saviour, and prepared to spend an eternity of joy with Him who hath redeemed them out of every nation, and kindred, and tribe; and with them the ransomed, gathered children of Abraham, His chosen nation now restored to favor.

To these, as occupants of the earth in its renewed condition, will be added a multitude of the nations of the earth, who shall have been spared the judgments inflicted upon the open and avowed enemies of Jesus. These gathered from every quarter, shall swell the number of those who will hail our Lord as their glorious, gracious Prince. Then shall be verified the precious assurance "that the heathen shall be given to Him for an inheritance, and the uttermost parts of the earth for a possession." Then also will be realized the enrapturing visions of favored prophets, and all the glowing, graphic descriptions of holy seers as they looked into the then distant future, and saw the heavenly scenes of millennial glory.

CHAPTER VIII.

CHARACTER OF THE PRESENT DISPENSATION—PRE-MILLENNIAL ADVENT—JUDGMENT.

"DISPENSATION," WHAT?—SEVERAL DISPENSATIONS—MIXED CHARACTER OF THE PRESENT—MORAL CONDITION OF THE WORLD—THIS A SEASON OF DISCIPLINE—MIXED CHARACTER TO CONTINUE—ELECTION OF GRACE—GOSPEL TO BE PREACHED FOR A WITNESS—SATAN THE GOD OF THIS DISPENSATION—SON OF MAN TO BE REVEALED BEFORE THE MILLENNIUM—THE JUDGMENT WHAT?—TWO PRE-EMINENTLY MARKED ACTS OF THE JUDGMENT.

Let both grow together until the harvest.—MATT. 13:30.

THIS is recognized as part of the instructive parable of "the tares and the wheat." A man is represented as sowing good seed in his field, and a malicious enemy as stealthily casting tares in among them. In due time both spring up. When it is discovered that bad plants are intermingled with the good, the servants ask if they shall go and gather out the noxious weeds? "Let both *grow together until the harvest*," is the response. Then the separation would be made, and the tares be bound in bundles and burned up. The parable was designed to show the present state of things, and what is to be its ending; as plainly appears from the explanation given by the Divine Teacher Himself, and which will be made manifest by a consideration of,

I. The Moral Condition of the Present Age, or Dispensation;

II. The Coming of the Son of man to Effect a Change; and

III. The Judgment.

I. The Moral Condition of the Present Age, or Dispensation.

By the term "dispensation," as used in this connection, is meant a particular form of the Divine administration of the "Church and of the world, in relation to the Church, or the scheme or plan of God's dealings with men." The past six thousand years, or nearly that, of our world's history, presents us with several dispensations, each bearing its distinctive characteristics. "These dispensations," remarks the late Hon. Joel Jones, "are among the grandest themes of the Bible. They are stages or parts of an infinite scheme, which join on to others, yet hidden deep in the Divine mind. (Ephes. 2:7.) They were all appointed and arranged by God the Son. They are upheld and unfolded by His power for the ever increasing display of the Divine attributes." There are, strictly speaking, two great dispensations.[1] The first is that of which we

[1] Dr. Cummings enumerates six different dispensations, (more properly seven,) each ending in specific judgments. 1. The

have but a brief notice, which was very limited in its duration, but which was marked by the perfect absence of all physical and moral evil. It was the dispensation of Paradise, during which the great Creator looked with complacency on the work that He had wrought. It was marked by a particular mode of the Divine administration adapted to the existing state of things. How long this continued we are not informed. It was brief, however, in duration, and was ended by Adam's fearful apostacy. Sin, at the instigation of Satan, was introduced, and the whole aspect of our earth and the whole character of man, and consequently the Divine administration, were essentially changed. A curse fell upon the earth for man's sake. It became subject to vanity and corruption, and with man, now degenerate and depraved, with the frown of insulted heaven upon his soul, it was made to groan and travail in pain even to this present hour. This has been aptly termed the dispensation of the fall, or curse. It covers several subordinate dispensations.[1] Such as the patriarchal, which, embracing

Adamic, which ended in retribution, as Adam and Eve were driven from Paradise. 2. The Antediluvian or Patriarchal, terminating also in judgment at the Deluge. 3. The Noachian, ending in the burning of Sodom and Gomorrah. 4. The Abrahamic, ending in judgments upon Egypt and the overthrow of Pharaoh. 5. The Mosaic, closing with the destruction of Jerusalem and the dispersion of the Jewish nation. 6. The present, to end with the coming of the Son of man in judgment upon the wicked. And we may add, 7. The Millennial.

[1] Jones.

the whole family of man, continued from Adam to the flood, and subsequently to the flood onward to the time of Moses; and which, indeed, continued to be the dispensation under which all the nations were placed, except the divinely chosen descendants of Jacob. "In respect to the posterity of Jacob, this [the Patriarchal] economy ended, at their exodus from Egypt, under the leadership of Moses, and the giving of the law at Mount Sinai. That people were then brought into new covenant relations with God; and thenceforth were regarded as a peculiar and elect people;" and the divine administration over them had its distinguishing characteristics. That was the Mosaic or Jewish dispensation, established over but a small portion of the human family, and continuing until the death of Christ, when, at that mysterious rending of the vail in the Temple, as the dying sufferer exclaimed, "It is finished!" the intimation was given that another dispensation had commenced; a dispensation still existing, and known as that of the Spirit. These former subordinate dispensations have been remedial in their nature, as is the present; having more or less direct reference to the curse of sin and its removal. Each was preparatory to the other; each was introduced by miraculous demonstrations; each was closed with Divine judgments; and each successive one unfolded more and more of the Divine purposes of mercy, touching the redemption of the earth and its occupants from the curse. The dispensation under which we live is that of the fall or curse, while it is that of the Spirit in its subordinate division.

These subordinate periods, the Patriarchal, the Mosaic, and that of the Spirit, differing in many things (each having its characteristic features of God's dealing with, or administration over those living under it), have, notwithstanding, in common, one prominent feature, belonging to the dispensation of the fall. It is the character of mixed or intermingled good and evil, with a sad preponderance, however, of the element of evil. It is of much importance that this feature of the existing dispensation be well considered, inasmuch as it has a direct bearing upon another—a coming dispensation of a totally different character, but to which it is preparatory. The expression of the parable, "Let *both* grow together until the harvest," has primary reference to the righteous and the wicked, the children of God and the children of the evil one, intermixed under the present economy, intermingled in all the relations of life, intermingled indeed in the visible Church. But it embraces, also, the good and the evil of individual character—the inconsistencies, and imperfections, and sins of believers—coexisting with holy affections and a life of godliness. And, also, the varied experience of the good and evil, the joy and sorrow, the hopes and fears, the peace and anxiety, the lights and shadows of every-day life, constituting the sum of earthly enjoyment and the sum of earthly trial. This life is a checkered scene. In the wise but mysterious providence of God, when man fell from his original state of purity and bliss, by which was ended the dispensation of Paradise, Satan, through whose immediate agency the ruin was effected, and by whom sin was introduced into our world, was permitted to usurp authority, such as to entitle him to the emphatic and significant designations of "the god of this world;" "the prince of this world;" "the prince of the power of the air;" "the spirit that now worketh in the children of disobedience."

By the fall of man, Satan, in a sense, gained a signal triumph. It was permitted in the wisdom of God that it might be overruled to His greater glory. Satan has ever striven to retain the ascendency. And here again has he been permitted to succeed, so far as to render but very partial the influences instituted, in the mercy of God, to remove and banish sin and sorrow from the earth.[1] For nearly six thousand years have good and evil coexisted. "Christianity," it has been well remarked,[2] "does not exist alone in the world. It stands in the midst of rival religions, the inventions of Satan or of men instigated and controlled by him." There exist two great opposing powers, the Spirit of the Living God, and Satan; and two controlling systems, the Gospel of Christ, and false religion in its varied forms. "The Church of Christ does not stand alone as an organized body, striving to draw all men to

[1] See chap. v.

[2] D. Lord.

itself to make them partakers of its faith and sharers in its hopes. It is surrounded, on every hand, by antagonistic organizations, which are endeavoring to extend their sway, or to maintain their dominion over the minds and the hearts of their deluded subjects. Satan has a kingdom in this world as well as Christ, and he is allowed to exert his gigantic powers in efforts to maintain it, by drawing to his side vast crowds of evil men—in making human governments his instruments, and in rendering learning, art, worldly science and wealth subservient to his cause. And he has carried his conquests into the Church itself. Evil is as predominant as it was fifteen centuries ago. It has as deep a hold on the human mind; it enters as largely into the institutions of society; it has as numerous and powerful engines at work in sustaining and extending its sway, relatively to the evangelical Church, as at former periods."[1] At every step in its attempted onward progress, the religion of the Cross meets with corresponding opposition. The devil's grand purpose is utterly to destroy the beneficent, saving influence of the Gospel, if perchance he can; or, if not daring presumptuously to anticipate such a result, his effort is to impair and check that influence to the utmost of Satanic ability. It is his aim and settled purpose not only to prevent, if so he may, by any artifice or power, the extension of the Gospel among men, but also to check the

[1] See chap. v.

increase of godliness, and to mar the beauty of holiness, and to stay the spiritual enjoyment of individual Christian experience. Hence the ceaseless temptations to which believers are exposed. Hence the need of constant, prayerful watchfulness against the wiles of the adversary.

The Christian's present life is emphatically a conflict; and although ultimately successful, yet subject to repeated discomfitures, as Satan gains temporary advantage. This is a system of trial and of discipline. It is designed, in part, to be a test of character, and it is for the development of Christian character, good and evil, under the influence, on the one hand, of the Spirit of God, and on the other, of Satan, the prince of darkness. Man, under the trials to which he is subjected is led to act out his real principles—to develop his dispositions—to show just what is the true character of his affections towards God, and to prove his fitness or unfitness for the Kingdom of righteousness. "And the result of this experiment is the demonstration, on a vast, appalling scale, of the utter indisposition of men spontaneously to return to God, and the hopelessness of their redemption, unless it be under an administration in which the great agents which now tempt them to evil, shall be precluded from exerting on them their deluding, maddening power, and the Spirit of God take exclusive and absolute possession of their hearts." Thus in the condition and character of the world, and in the individual experience of the people of God, is the present dispensation one of commingled good and evil—one of wheat and tares growing together. "Let both grow together *until the harvest.*"

A time is predicted of the Church and of the world, when a grand change shall be effected, touching character and condition, when there shall no longer be permitted the intermingling of good and evil—when every baleful, sinister element shall be taken out from that which is good, and when influences shall be exerted, uninterfered with and unimpaired, to make the subjects of them truly blessed and perfectly holy. A time it will be—when Satan, the author and instigator of all this evil, shall be bound, so that he can no more, for a predicted period, work out his purposes of mischief—a time when this earth, renewed and freed from the thraldom under which it shall have groaned since the curse first fell upon it, will be made an appropriate dwelling-place for the risen, ransomed, glorified saints, and the Church of the Living God, under the immediate government of the Redeemer. In the meantime, or up to that period, the second advent of Christ, this intermixture of good and evil, with, it would appear an increasing preponderance of evil, seems to be the predicted character of the dispensation under which we live. Our earth is not gradually becoming more and more freed from the dominion of the god of this world. The subjects of his government are not becoming relatively smaller in number as the months and years and centuries advance. For it is worthy of special notice that the tares are not to be removed from the wheat by any gradual process. The prevalent teaching on the subject of the Millennium would seem, however, to imply that the tares are actually to be gradually *converted into wheat*, rather than separated from them that they may be "*burned*." For the promised state of righteousness is to be brought about, we are told, by the gradual spread of Gospel truth, subduing all hearts to itself, changing the evil into the good—the tares into wheat! Such is far from being the doctrine of the parable. In the time of harvest, or at the end of the world or dispensation, the Son of man shall send forth His angels, and they shall gather out of His Kingdom all things that offend, just as the reapers are to gather the tares and burn them in the fire. Satan will hold his full supremacy until the descent of the angel from heaven, having the key of the bottomless pit, and a great chain in his hand, and laying hold of the arch apostate, will bind him and cast him into the abyss.

Although he is to retain his dominion here until that period comes, he cannot frustrate the grand purpose of the Lord—a purpose of mercy, for which especially, it may be, the present dispensation is perpetuated yet a little; a dispensation which is to gather in from the nations of the earth His elect people—the chosen heirs of everlasting life. This has been the gracious procedure of God since the time the first soul was regenerated. Although the earth was blighted and the race of apostate man ruined by sin, yet all were not ultimately to perish. And from Adam to our own day has He been gathering into His fold the subjects of His elective love. At all times has He had a seed to serve Him—a people brought out from amid His enemies, and drawn by sovereign grace and love to Himself.

To St. Paul, yielding to despondency, and seemingly about to abandon his post of duty, as he labored amid Corinthian opposers, the Lord spoke in a vision and said; "Be not afraid, but speak, and hold not thy peace, for I am with thee, and no man shall set on thee to hurt thee; *for I have much people in this city.*" (Acts 18:9,10.) These subjects of His elective love, these "much people" were pagans at the time, but they were to be gathered in, and to this end Paul must speak to them the words of eternal life. It is said of the divine Redeemer, as upon one occasion He was about to go from Judea into Galilee; "*He must needs go through Samaria.*" (John 4:4.) And wherein consisted the "needs be" or the necessity to pass that way? This was not the usual route between the two districts. Indeed, it was generally carefully avoided, because of the enmity existing between the Jews and Samaritans. They were accustomed to cross over Jordan near Jericho, and passing up the river on its eastern side, recross into Galilee after getting beyond the territory of the hated Samaritans. Wherefore then must Christ needs go through Samaria?

In the purposes of Heaven it was designed that

a certain woman of that place, and some of her countrymen, should be made subjects of redeeming love. They were of the election of grace. This was the purposed time of their salvation, and Christ Jesus was to bear them the tidings of mercy. Hence must the divine Teacher "needs go through Samaria." An Ethiopian eunuch, a man high in authority under Candace, the queen, was returning from Jerusalem, whither he had gone to worship at the feast. He was also a chosen subject of Heaven's eternal love, and hence must be brought to a knowledge of the truth. Philip was commissioned by an angel of the Lord to go down from Jerusalem towards Gaza, thus to accomplish the divine purpose. Overtaking the distinguished man as, riding in his chariot, he read Esaias, the prophet, he made known unto him Him of whom the prophet wrote. The eunuch in faith received Him—was baptized, and went on his way rejoicing, and no doubt anxious to communicate the glad tidings of salvation to others in the spiritually benighted land to which he went.[1] (Acts 8.)

The Apostle Peter (Acts 15 : 14) declared that "God did visit the *Gentiles to take out of them* [OR FROM AMONG THEM] *a people for His name;*" and said that he was chosen to preach to the Gentiles, that he might select out, or rather, that

[1] In Ethiopia, a region south of Egypt, Christianity existed at an early period, and tradition gives to this converted eunuch, the credit of introducing it there; Neander, however, questions the correctness of the tradition.

the grace of God, through his instrumentality, might bring out from among the sinful pagan nations, His chosen ones. Thus has it been to the present time, and more especially in these latter days, is the proclamation of the Gospel made, as never before, so that already it has been heard by almost every nation under heaven; and vast multitudes at home and abroad, have been made the trophies of redeeming grace. They are the Lord's elect children, and must needs be gathered into the fold. But while all this is in the process of accomplishment, the wheat and the tares grow together as heretofore. The dispensation does not change its characteristic feature. Good and evil continue intermingled—the relative proportion of tares not diminishing. It remains a dispensation of trial and of discipline—a season of conflicting interests—one of opposing, antagonistic powers and influences. And thus the Scriptures teach us will it be up to the very close of the dispensation. As Satan is now, so he will be "the god of this world," even unto the end. His influence is to be predominant. Now mark the expression, "*god of this world.*" The essential difference between the words in the original of the New Testament, both of which are rendered in our translation, "world," has been already noticed. They are "kosmos," the material, physical earth in its visible arrangement, and "aion," period or age. The word in this passage is the latter. Satan is the god of this period or dispensation—a time of limited duration, during which he is permitted to mingle the evil with the good. And he will remain such even to its close, when bound by the angel, he will be imprisoned in the bottomless pit for a thousand years. And as a consequence the present dispensation of commingled evil and good will be succeeded by one of righteousness and joy. The wheat and the tares are to remain *until* the *harvest*, when the reapers shall be bidden to gather, first the tares and bind them in bundles to burn them, and the wheat shall be gathered into the garners of the Master. But what is meant by the *harvest?* The field is the world, "kosmos," this material world or earth on which we dwell. The *enemy* who sowed the tares is the devil. The *harvest* is the end of the "aion," the end of the age or dispensation. And then, at the *harvest*, shall be gathered out of His Kingdom all things that offend, and them that do iniquity, and shall be cast into a furnace of fire.

The advent of that time is intimately associated with the fulfilment of another assurance given by the Saviour; "This Gospel of the Kingdom shall be preached in all the world for a *witness* unto all nations; and *then shall the end come.*" (Matt. 24:14.) The Gospel shall be preached to all nations, not for their universal or general conversion, but for a very different purpose. Nowhere in the Word of God, is the conversion of the nations said to be the object of the great commission to preach the Gospel to every creature. It shall be preached "for a witness." It shall be proclaimed in testimony of God's infinite mercy, in the provisions of His grace, and *then*, this having been accomplished, shall the *end* come. And what *end?* The end of the times of the Gentiles—the end of the treading down of Jerusalem—the end of Satan's dominion—the end of the present dispensation. And that will be at the time of the promised second advent of the Son of man.

We have already had occasion to consider, to some extent, the question of the time of the personal coming of Christ, in its relation to the Millennium, and whether this glorious era is to be brought about by the gradual spread of Gospel truth, or to be inaugurated by the Redeemer in person, as He shall come to destroy all evil from the earth and make it a blessed abode for the righteous. The signs of the times appear plainly to indicate that this great question is soon to have its full solution in the actual accomplishment of predicted events; and the importance of them will warrant a brief reference to it again, as it is so intimately connected with the subject just discussed. As stated in a previous discussion, all expect a personal second advent of our Lord. The Scriptures are full of assurances to this effect. But *when* will He come? Will it be before or after the Millennium? We will consider then as proposed,

II. The Pre-millennial Advent of Christ.[1]

If we are taught by the Word of God that the

[1] Chapters 5 and 9.

present state of things—the existence, and even the predominance of evil in our world is to continue—if the tares and the wheat are not to be separated until the end of this world or dispensation—if Satan is the god of this world or age, implying the continuance of his dominion and widespread influence *until its close*, then surely are we to look for the predicted coming of the Son of man before the Millennium, inasmuch as these evils must be removed before that period can be enjoyed, and their removal is to be effected by the advent of the Saviour, and by the binding of Satan at His coming. If the man of sin, the antichrist, the offspring of a combination of the papal mystery of iniquity with atheistic powers, is to be destroyed *before* the Millennium can commence, then must Christ come *before* that time of blessedness; as it is by the brightness of His coming, or by the fiery manifestation of His appearing, that this gigantic evil is to end. If, as Daniel in his seventh chapter declares; One like the Son of man is to *come with the clouds of heaven* to receive *dominion and glory and a kingdom*, that all people, nations and languages should serve Him; whose dominion is an everlasting dominion, which shall not pass away; and whose Kingdom that which shall not be destroyed; and if that Kingdom is to be established on the destruction of the fourth beast, or the fourth kingdom, (the Roman empire still in its divided condition on the Continent of Europe), and if that fourth kingdom is to end before the Millennium, then must this coming of one "like the Son of man with the clouds of heaven," be before the Millennium. If there is to be a resurrection of the holy dead at the commencement of the thousand years, and if, as Paul assures us, the dead in Christ are to rise first, at the coming of the Lord, and if these risen saints are to live and reign with Christ a thousand years, then the visible, personal coming of the Son of man must be before the thousand years. If the children of Judah and of Israel are to remain in their wide dispersion, under the manifested displeasure of their covenant God, with their holy city trodden down, UNTIL the times of the Gentiles be fulfilled; and if the restoration to their forfeited blessedness, the repossession of their lost inheritance, and the destruction of their enemies, are to precede and to usher in the Millennium; then will the coming of Christ be before that period, because, as the inspired evangelist informs us, the redemption of this people, Israel, is to take place at the time of Christ's coming. That redemption is to be amid scenes of fearful commotion. And "*then* shall they see the Son of man coming in a cloud with power and great glory. *And when these things begin to come to pass then look up and lift up your heads*, FOR YOUR REDEMPTION DRAWETH NIGH." (Luke 21 : 27, 28.) Thus we are taught to expect this glorious event, the second coming of the Son of man, before the Millennium, and for it are ever to watch, and in the anticipation of it are ever to rejoice. With ten thousands of His saints shall He come, to execute judgment upon the wicked, and to be glorified in His saints. This will be the commencement, or the morning of that grand eventful period known as

III. The Day of Judgment.

The period which this covers and the idea that it expresses, are very different in the minds of those who are looking for the speedy and personal advent of the Saviour, from those maintained by such as have no such anticipation. The latter refer it to the closing up of all human things—the ending of time. They teach us that it is, exclusively, the scene described at the close of the twentieth chapter of the Revelation, when the Judge is to come, seated on His great white throne; is to have gathered before Him the risen dead of all generations, and of every character; and when they shall be rewarded according to their respective deserts; the righteous to be acquitted and glorified; and the wicked to be condemned, and with the devil, the beast, and the false prophet, and everything that offends, to be "cast into the lake of fire." And it is by such believed that the period embraced is very limited in duration, if it be not confined to that of a literal day of twenty-four hours. The former believe it to be a protracted period, having its opening scene at the visible coming of the Son of man at the beginning of the Millennium, to continue through that season, and to close with the trial, condemnation, and punishment of the then risen wicked of all past centuries, together with Satan and his confederates in wickedness. This is the important question we are now briefly to consider. It is of moment to decide between opinions so widely at variance. What are we, then, to understand by the "*day of Judgment?*" Many readers of the Bible know the somewhat painful perplexities they have experienced in anticipating this eventful "day;" as they supposed it to embrace the period of a natural day, or one at most of very limited continuance. They have been led to inquire; How can these stupendous events, the individual trial and judgment of the myriads of the family of Adam, and the host of angelic beings, fallen and unfallen—of all, indeed, who shall have passed a season of probation, be crowded in so brief a period? True is it, indeed, if such be the revelation of the Most High, we may safely leave the solution of the difficulty with Him. But all perplexity is at an end, when we adopt what we believe to be the true scriptural import of the phrase.

What is meant by "day" in this expression? We believe it to be a period of very protracted duration. It is hardly necessary to dwell upon the fact, that the term is thus very frequently used in the word of God. It is a well-known fact, that many of the most eminent geologists ascribe to the several "days" of creation a period of indefinite duration. Each day covers thousands and thousands of years. We moreover read of the "day of vengeance," "the day of salvation," (the protracted period of offered mercy,) "the day of visitation," &c. And thus are we accustomed to use it in ordinary conversation. It is used to designate periods characterized by the existence of persons of marked distinction and influence, as well as to designate characteristic periods in the history of a particular people or the world. Thus, what is more common than to speak of Cromwell's day, of Washington's day, of Bonaparte's day,—referring to the times in which these lived, and embracing a more or less protracted period. We also speak of the "day of despotism," the "day of freedom," the "day of barbarism," the "day of refined literature;" each also embracing a period of more or less duration—it may be of years, or even centuries. Thus no objection lies against the interpretation we put upon the word in this connection, "the *day* of Judgment." We believe it to imply a period of at least one thousand years. What, then, is the *Judgment?* Are the acts of trial, of acquittal, of condemnation, of rewards and punishment, to be continued through this extended period? We answer, no; and state that the inquiry is based on a fundamental error, as we understand it, of the scriptural meaning of "Judgment." The ordinary conception of the term has been that of trial and of sentence, before and by a judge seated on his tribunal in court, or at an assize. This idea, in reference to procedure in human governments, is transferred to the Divine administration. Whereas the scriptural idea of a *Judge* is very different. It is not so much that of a Jurist on the bench as that of a Ruler. He is a *King*, or one in authority to govern and to rule, to deliver and protect his people, and to avenge them of their enemies. This character and office of such Rulers is clearly exhibited in the history of "The Judges," raised up by the Lord for deliverers and avengers. When the people demanded a *King*, it was not with a view to change the *nature* of the office; but impiously to cast off the recognition of their immediate dependence on Jehovah, and to be like the surrounding nations. Their demand was, "Make us a *King* to *judge* us." "We will have a King over us, that we also may be like all the nations, and that our *King* may *judge* us, and go out before us and fight our battles." (1 Sam. 8:19, 20.) The Scriptures, speaking of judgment, very frequently connect with it the idea of general government and control. "Oh, let the nations be glad and sing for joy; for Thou shalt *judge* the people righteously, and *govern* the nations upon earth." (Ps. 67:4.) And so is it in a passage having direct reference to the Lord Jesus Christ Himself. "Unto us a Son is given, and the *government* shall be upon His shoulder. . . . Of the increase of His *government and peace* there shall be no end upon the *throne* of David, and upon His kingdom, to order it and to establish it with *judgment* and with justice forever." (Isaiah 9:6.) "Behold, a *King* shall *reign* and prosper, and shall execute *judgment* and justice in the earth." (Jer. 23:5.) Such is the import of judgeship in the Bible. It is that of government or rule, and the administration of justice. It is the management of affairs under the control of a ruling prince.

Hence, when the Scriptures speak of the "Day of Judgment," they speak, as we understand it, of the administration of our Lord, as Ruler during the whole period of the Millennium, and onwards to the closing scene of Rev. 20:11. It will be commenced at His promised visible appearing as Avenger and Judge of His people. It will be continued through the predicted period of a thousand years, during which the government shall be "upon His shoulder," as supreme Judge or Ruler. And then the last effort of Satanic and human wickedness will be put forth; which, issuing in the utter overthrow of the conspirators, will lead to the final act of retributive justice—to the eternal expulsion of Satan and his host from the earth—to the passing of the sentence, and infliction of punishment upon the risen wicked dead of all preceding ages, and the establishment of the eternal state of peace, glory, and felicity for the righteous.

Thus there will be *two pre-eminently marked acts of the Judgment.* The one will be at the end of the present age; and is that foreshadowed by the "harvest" in the parable of the "tares and wheat," when the Son of man shall send forth His angels to execute His judgments upon the living wicked, and when "the righteous shall shine forth as the sun in the kingdom of their Father." (Matt. 13.) Scenes foreshadowed, also, by the parable of the "net," and by the gathering together, also, of the existing nations for judgment, as described, Matt.

25. Then, moreover, will be verified the assurance of the Apostle: "The Lord shall be revealed from heaven, ... in flaming fire, taking vengeance on them that know not God, and that obey not the Gospel of our Lord Jesus Christ, who shall be punished with everlasting destruction. . . . . And when He shall be glorified in His saints, and admired in all them that believe." (2 Thess. 1:7.)

This *first* act of the eventful drama will consist of *two distinct scenes.* The first embracing the judgment of the righteous—the risen pious dead of generations past, and all who, living at the time, shall be prepared to meet their Lord in peace. The second scene—between which and the first there may be, for aught we know, some considerable period of time[1]—will be the Judgment of the living nations as described in Matt. 25. The second grand act in the process of Judgment to which we alluded, is referred to at the close of the twentieth chapter of the Revelation, and of the scenes of which we have just spoken. Thus this "Day of Judgment" will have its *morning* and its *evening*, like any other day. Its morning will be ushered in by the coming of the Son of man; and the dawning of that morning will be the appearance of the significant "signs" which are to precede His advent. Its evening will be the period when Satan, death, the risen wicked, and all that shall have disturbed and

[1] See chap. 10.

polluted the earth, shall be given over to the "second death." The twilight of that evening auguring its fearful coming, will be the last effort of Satan, with his confederate host, against the "saints and the beloved city."

CHAPTER IX.

SECOND ADVENT—ITS NATURE—TIME—AND PRACTICAL BEARING.

THINGS UNREVEALED NOT PROPER SUBJECTS OF SPECULATION—STUDY OF UNFULFILLED PROPHECY A PRIVILEGE AND A DUTY—OBJECTION CONSIDERED—NATURE OF CHRIST'S SECOND COMING—A SPIRITUAL COMING—A PROVIDENTIAL, A LITERAL AND PERSONAL COMING—PROPHETS ANTICIPATED IT—CHRIST'S TWOFOLD CHARACTER—SCRIPTURAL EXPRESSIONS FOR SECOND ADVENT—TIME OF SECOND ADVENT, RELATIVE AND SPECIFIC—PRACTICAL BEARING OF THE DOCTRINE—DEATH NOT THE SCRIPTURAL MOTIVE TO HOLY LIVING—PROFESSOR HACKETT'S TESTIMONY—SPECIMENS OF SCRIPTURAL APPEALS.

A more sure word of prophecy, whereunto ye do well that ye take heed.—2 PET. 1 : 19.

This same Jesus which is taken up from you into heaven, shall so come in like manner as ye have seen Him go into heaven.—ACTS 1 : 11.

All Scripture is profitable for righteousness.—2 TIM. 3 : 16.

NOT only are the truths revealed in the Bible the inspiration of the Holy Spirit, but they are designed for our spiritual good. It is through the truth that we are sanctified. Error is always injurious in its tendency. All Scripture is profitable. There is nothing contained in these divine oracles which may not be made available to our spiritual welfare. Some truths are of a more decidedly practical nature than others; but all are to be received and studied, that they may produce their legitimate results, in moulding moral character, and fitting us the better for duty here, and for the experience and enjoyment of what is to be revealed hereafter. Mere speculation or conjecture can be of but little profit. Much time may be spent in endeavoring to unravel mysteries; much in striving to comprehend or discover what lies beyond the reach of our comprehension, or what is not properly within the range of our investigation, and which cannot be discovered, because it has not been revealed. All such time and effort are vainly expended. There is much in the future hidden from our view; and it is not for man to strive to penetrate, or to uplift the vail which shuts out from vision these unrevealed portions of God's wise and wondrous plan. Patiently must we wait for their revelation, as He shall unfold and develop His purposes, more and more clearly, for the admiration and blessedness of His Church. There are, however, things pertaining to the future, which the Lord has been pleased clearly to make known. Prophecy is a prominent feature of the Bible record, and it is given to us for our edification and study. Much of the prophetic Scriptures has already met with its literal fulfilment, and much remains yet to be fulfilled; while each day, as it passes by, presents us with predictions in the actual process of accomplishment.

Prophecy, already fulfilled, confirms our confidence in the truthfulness of the Scriptures and in the faithfulness of God. It is a standing proof of the truth of the religion of the Bible, which infidelity vainly strives to gainsay, or to successfully resist; and it is the assurance, moreover, that what remains unfulfilled will as certainly be verified. But is the study of unfulfilled prophecy a profitable study? Is it a subject of legitimate investigation? May we not be benefited by what is already accomplished, and leave what is future without special inquiry or care, and especially so because of the conflicting views of professed interpreters in regard to many of these predictions? So some reason, and so some regulate their course, persuading themselves that the study of what is not fulfilled is not for edification or instruction. This is not, however, in accordance with the Spirit, or the teachings of the word of God; for *all* Scripture is not only given by inspiration, but is also "profitable."

The prophets, in former days, carefully studied the predictions they were bidden themselves to deliver. "Of which salvation the prophets have inquired and searched diligently, who prophesied of the grace that should come unto you, searching what, or what manner of time, the Spirit of Christ, which was in them did signify, when it testified beforehand the sufferings of Christ and the glory that should follow." (1 Pet. 1:10, 11.) If they were thus employed, wishing to understand the import of their own words, surely the prayerful examination of what the Lord declares to be yet in reserve for the world and the Church, is not only a duty but a privilege; inasmuch as scenes far more glorious and startling than have ever transpired on earth are before us, and it may be not far removed. A special blessing is pronounced on those who make these coming events the subject of inquiry. The volume of inspiration closes with the most extended and intricate portion of the prophetic writings; and at the very opening of the "Revelation" we hear the inspired Apostle saying, as it were in anticipation of any objection to the study which might be raised, and for the encouragement of the inquirer; "*Blessed* is he that readeth, and they that hear the words of this prophecy and keep those things which are written therein; for the time is at hand." (Rev. 1:3.) Thus would the Spirit of the Lord lead us to examine those things of the future which have been made the subjects of revelation. It is to be done with a docile, prayerful, unprejudiced spirit, if we would secure the promised blessedness.

It should be remembered, moreover, that *all* are *actually* interpreters of predictions not yet fulfilled. Even those who are disposed to question the expediency and profitableness of the study of unaccomplished prophecies have their several systems of interpretation, in reference to the prominent events of the future. Now the great question is, whether or not these systems be correct—whether or not their interpretations be legitimate? And the inquiry is of greatest importance, and it is just that to which we earnestly desire to draw attention.

Thus our belief of a Millennium—of the resurrection—of the Judgment—of the personal coming of Christ—of an eternity of blessedness for the righteous, and of misery for the wicked, is from unfulfilled prophecy. We believe these things because the Scriptures declare they *shall* be. They are the subjects of prophecies *yet* to be fulfilled. Now the great question, we say, has respect to the correctness of our interpretation. Thus we believe in a coming Millennium; but are our views of that Millennium scriptural? Is it to be secured by the gradual diffusion of light and truth; and that by instrumentalities now employed, until all nations shall be brought into subjection to the cross? Or is it to be preceded by great and startling revolutions and commotions, the world being still under the dominion of the demon god of this dispensation, until by signal, Divine manifestations of Almighty power, sudden destruction shall come upon the opposing nations of the earth, and upon all that shall be found arrayed against the Gospel of Christ Jesus—thus ushering in the day of millennial glory? How does the word of God decide *this* question? Is our cherished interpretation on this point correct? All evangelical Christians believe in a *resurrection*. We thus, again, interpret unfulfilled prophecy. But are our views on *this* subject scriptural? Is that resurrection to be a simultaneous, promiscuous uprising, from their resting-places, of the bodies of the dead, both righteous and wicked, of all generations past, embracing every dispensation—the thousand years of promised blessedness, and all time up to the supposed coming of Christ, who then, at the closing of earth's drama, will appear in judgment and annihilate the globe? Or, is there to be a resurrection of the pious dead, known as the *first* resurrection, at the *commencement* of the Millennium, while "the rest of the dead" are not to live, or be raised, until the thousand years shall be passed, when the destiny of the ungodly will be finally and forever sealed? What is the scriptural doctrine on *this* subject? Which interpretation of unfulfilled prophecy will stand the test of careful investigation? We believe that the kingdom of the Redeemer is to be established here below, and that Christ Jesus will, at some time, personally and visibly return to this very earth. This we believe, because prophecy, *yet* to be fulfilled, clearly reveals it. But is the kingdom of the Redeemer, which is here to be set up, to be an exclusively spiritual kingdom, He reigning, by His Holy Spirit in the hearts of believers, but not to appear personally until that kingdom of a thousand years shall be closed, when He will come to judge and to declare the destinies of men? Or will He visibly come before the Millennium, to reign here personally with His risen, glorified saints, establishing His kingdom, not only spiritually in the hearts of His people, but personally to rule over the ransomed nations of our world? These are some of the questions to be settled. Not whether or no we will give attention to unfulfilled prophecy, for this we already do; but whether or not the interpretation we do actually give to the predictions is correct? A question only to be answered by a careful and candid examination of the Scriptures, and one, confessedly, which involves interests of the greatest importance.

Prominent amid the subjects of inquiry is that of the SECOND COMING OF OUR LORD JESUS CHRIST. We have already, in our previous discussions, taken occasion frequently to refer to it. Our present object is, although briefly, yet more particularly than we have done, to consider it:

I. IN ITS NATURE.

II. IN ITS TIME; AND

III. IN ITS PRACTICAL BEARINGS.

I. AS TO ITS NATURE.

There is a spiritual coming of Christ spoken of in the Scriptures. Said the Saviour, "If a man love me, my Father will love him, and we will come unto him, and make our abode with him." (John 14 : 23.) "Behold, I stand at the door and knock: if any man hear My voice and open the door, I will come in to him, and will sup with him and he with Me." (Rev. 3 : 20.) This is, unquestionably, a spiritual coming, and it is one in which every regenerated soul has a special interest. So may there be said to be a *providential* coming of Jesus. Every providence that affects our weal or woe—every startling incident of life, may, in a sense, be said to be the coming of Him whose ordering it is. So the solemn warning to the church at Sardis; "If, therefore, thou shalt not watch, I will come on thee as a thief, and thou shalt not know what hour I will come upon thee." (Rev. 3:3.) But these, the spiritual and providential comings of Christ, are not what are meant by the emphatic and repeated assurances of the "coming of the Son of man."

The prophets of old, in glowing strains, spoke of the advent of the Messiah—Israel's Prince and Deliverer. And ardent were the anticipations which these animating predictions awakened. The character of the predicted One was twofold. He was described by Isaiah as a suffering victim of bitter persecution—"A man of sorrows and acquainted with grief; despised and rejected of men." He was also described as a ruling Prince, a gloriously exalted King upon His throne, whose dominion should extend over the earth, and whose dominion should know no end. There was to be given unto Him, as Daniel declares, "dominion, glory, and a *kingdom*, that all people, nations, and languages should *serve* Him. His dominion is an everlasting dominion which shall not pass away, and His kingdom that which shall not be destroyed." Thus the range of the prophet's vision embraced more than the advent of Christ eighteen hundred years since, when as the helpless babe, at Bethlehem, He appeared the incarnate One who came on His mission of mercy to our perishing race; and when, as man's atoning sacrifice, He hung, a murdered Nazarene, upon the cross. This was His state of humiliation and of suffering; and was the verification of only a part of the prediction. That prediction extended onward for many centuries, and embraced a *second* coming, when should be realized the visions of a glorious Prince in possession of a dominion and a kingdom over all people, and nations, and languages—a dominion that was to be everlasting, and a kingdom "without end." The prophecy had respect to a reigning Prince, as well as to a suffering victim. As one part of the prediction did not mean a spiritual coming, but a personal, literal advent to suffer and to die, so neither does the other—or that yet waiting its fulfilment, which regards Him as a ruling Prince on earth—admit of a spiritual or figurative interpretation. It is to be a visible, personal advent, as certainly as was that when eastern Magi offered their gifts in the lowly abode at Bethlehem; or when the diseased and demon-possessed of Jerusalem knew His healing power; or when scoffing priests reviled the sufferer on the cross; or when wondering disciples saw Him pass from their vision, as they gazed up from Olivet into the opened heavens. "This same Jesus which is taken from you into heaven, shall so come in like manner as ye have seen Him go into heaven." So spake the angels to the disciples, and their words will assuredly be verified. He was *seen* to go into heaven, and so will he be *seen* to come again. "This *same* Jesus;" and in *like manner*, as he *went* will He *return*. Here can be nothing less than a personal, visible advent. Nor are the words to wait for their literal fulfilment until the Millennium be passed.

It may be a matter of some interest to note the *manner* in which the Scriptures are wont to speak of the second advent of Christ. This will give us additional proof that such advent cannot be a spiritual or a figurative coming. This coming is represented by at least twelve different words or expressions, and these occur about one hundred and twenty-five times in undoubted reference to this great event. The import of three of these words would seem to settle the question touching the nature of the advent of the Redeemer. The first is a word which gives the title to the last book of the Scriptures, "The Revelation," sometimes called the Apocalypse of Christ—the Greek word "*Apokalupsis*," meaning revelation or manifestation. "The Revelation of Jesus Christ" is the beginning and the title of the book, because His personal coming, the revelation or manifestation of Himself, is its grand, prominent subject.[1] The word occurs in 1 Cor. 1:7, "waiting for the coming [the revelation, as the original is] of Jesus Christ." "When the Lord Jesus shall be revealed from heaven." (2 Thess. 1:7.) "At the appearing [revelation] of Jesus Christ." "Hope for the grace that is to be brought unto you at the revelation of Jesus Christ." (1 Pet. 1:7, 13.) A second word is "*Epiphania*," and means appearance—personal appearance. It occurs in 2 Tim.

[1] W. Newton.

1:10, in reference to the first coming of our Lord in the flesh, and in 1 Tim. 6:14, to His second coming, "until the appearing [epiphania] of our Lord Jesus Christ." "Who shall judge the quick and the dead at His appearing and His Kingdom," "unto all them that love His *appearing*." (2 Tim. 4:1, 8.) "Looking for that blessed hope and the glorious *appearing* of the Great God and (even) of our Saviour Jesus Christ." (Tit. 2:13.) The third word used is "*Parousia*," which embraces always the idea of personal presence, "arrival" (Donnegan). It is found four times in Matt. 24, in reference to the second advent of Christ. "What shall be the sign of Thy *coming*" [parousia]? "So shall the *coming* [parousia] of the Son of man be." "As the days of Noah were, so shall the *coming* [parousia] of the Son of man be." St. Paul thus uses the word "They that are Christ's at His *coming*." (1 Cor. 15:23.) "Are not even ye in the presence of our Lord Jesus Christ at His *coming*." (1 Thess. 2:19.) "At the *coming* of our Lord Jesus Christ with all His saints." (1 Thess. 3:13.) "We which are alive and remain unto the *coming* of the Lord." (1 Thess. 4:15.) Such are some of the passages where these words are used. In other places we find them in reference to *other* objects or persons, but never to denote a spiritual or figurative revelation or appearance or advent or presence. Always where it is an object of sense, a literal, personal, visible appearance is meant.

Thus nothing, surely, is more clearly revealed than the visible second coming of the Son of man to this very earth. On almost any page of the Bible is there reference, more or less direct, to it. It runs through the New Testament, as a golden thread, giving significancy and interest to every part, as it falls from the lips of the divine Teacher, or as it is spread out upon the pages of the epistles of the inspired apostles to the several Churches they addressed.

II. But, WHAT IS TO BE THE TIME OF HIS ADVENT? This is our *second* inquiry.

We have, in previous discussions, several times alluded to the coming of Christ as related to the Millennium; a frequency of reference justified by its paramount importance. We now again briefly consider it, preparatory to an examination of the question in reference to the more definite period of His advent.

In the Second Epistle of St. Paul to the Thessalonians, mention is made of "the man of sin," or the "antichrist," whose destruction is to be effected by the "brightness of the Lord's coming." It so happens that the *brightness* and the *coming* of this passage are, in the original, two of the words just referred to, each of which expresses the *personal appearance* of Him whose coming is spoken of. If neither of them when used singly can denote a spiritual advent, much less can they when conjoined; and if each of these, when employed separately, indubitably, means a *personal* and *corporeal* manifestation and presence, much more must they when united. The destruction of antichrist then is not to be a spiritual destruction, nor to be accomplished by any mere spiritual manifestation of his Destroyer. But his is to be a literal overthrow, effected by the brightness of the coming, or by the "appearance of the presence" of the Son of God in judgment on His enemies. There is also mention made in the same place, of the "mystery of iniquity," which was already working at the time St. Paul wrote his epistle. This "mystery," having its rudiments even in apostolic times, became under the development of subsequent ages, in its full manifestation, the formidable despotism which overshadowed Christendom, and was known as the all-controlling power whose seat was on the seven hills. It was the "scarlet clad woman," "the mother of abominations," the Romish hierarchy. The "man of sin" or the "antichrist," emphatically such, who is to appear in his full proportions immediately preceding the coming of Christ, is to be intimately related to this "mystery of iniquity." Now are "antichrist," the formidable "man of sin," and this power, impiously assuming the name of Christianity and the prerogatives of Christ—this gigantic evil—this grand antagonistic system of Satanic origin—to continue, as we have inquired once before, through the Millennium, and onward to a distant period—then to be destroyed at the predicted advent of the Lord Jesus, as He comes to judgment and to a world's annihilation? If not, then must that advent be before the Millennium. Both are to be destroyed at the "revelation" of the Son of God.

The same truth is revealed in the seventh of Daniel. We are, moreover taught, as has already been seen, that Satan is the "god of this world," or the god of this period (*aion*) or present dispensation; and here will he continue, by divine permission, to have the pre-eminence until the time shall have come for his being bound and cast into the abyss, previous to which the tares and the wheat are to remain intermingled, until the "harvest," which is the end of the world (*aion*)—the present dispensation or age, and then the Son of man shall come to make the grand separation, and to destroy the wicked, and to establish His Kingdom, which is to be the anticipated, longed-for thousand years of millennial blessedness. (Matt. 13: 39; Rev. 19 and 20.) The Gospel of the Kingdom is to be preached "for *a witness* unto all nations," in order that the Lord may take *out of them*—or out from among them—His elect people—"a people for His name;" and that every nation may have an opportunity to say, whether or not they will yield to the dominion of the Prince of righteousness.

Thus is the present period a period of suspended judgments—one of forbearance towards the guilty nations of the earth. But when the angel, bearing the everlasting Gospel, shall have accomplished his circuit of the globe, the time of forbearance shall cease—"the end shall come." "And *then* shall appear the sign of the Son of man in heaven, and then shall all the tribes of the earth mourn, and *they shall see the Son of man coming in the clouds of heaven*, with power and great glory. And He shall send His angels with a great sound of a trumpet, and they shall gather together His elect from the four winds, from one end of heaven to the other." (Matt. 24 : 30, 31.)

But the question as to the TIME OF THE SECOND ADVENT admits of, and seems to demand, a more definite answer; and we may consider,

1. *The relative period:*

2. *The specific or chronological time.*

Whatever may be thought and said by some of the presumption of those who venture to specify a particular "hour or day," or even year, wherein the Lord shall appear, we are, assuredly, warranted, yea, it is our enjoined *duty* so to consider the "signs" of His coming as at least to judge of our *proximate* nearness to the event; else the injunction is without meaning, "When these things [these signs just enumerated by the Saviour] begin to come to pass, then look up and lift up your heads, for your *redemption draweth nigh.*" (Luke 21 : 28.)

Various "signs" are specified, by which we are to judge of the near approach of the predicted period. And, if careful observers and attentive students are not greatly at fault in their calculations, based on these "signs," the time is near at hand, when a heedless world and a slumbering Church will be startled from their apathy by the cry; "*Behold! the Bridegroom cometh. Go ye out to meet Him.*" We are taught that these "signs" will be so clear a demonstration of the immediate coming and Kingdom of Christ, that we can know His coming is at hand, just as we know that summer is nigh when the trees begin to put forth leaves. (Lu. 21:30; Matt. 24:33.) We are not only taught to believe that we *can* know it, but we are as positively commanded to know it as we are to believe that Jesus is the Son of God. (Matt. 24:33; Ma. 13:29; Lu. 21:28, 31.) Among these "signs" immediately to precede this glorious event—the coming of our Lord—and by which we are to judge of its proximate nearness are:

1. *The Gospel is to be preached to all nations of the earth* "FOR A WITNESS." "This Gospel of the Kingdom shall be preached in all the world for a witness unto all nations; and then shall the end come." (Matt. 24:14; Acts 1:8.)

2. *A general apostasy from the faith in nominal Christendom.* "Nevertheless when the Son of man cometh shall He find faith on the earth?" (Lu. 18:8; 2 Thess. 2:3; 2 Tim. 3:1–5, 4:3–4, &c.)

3. *A great prevalence of iniquity in the world.* "As the days of Noah were, so shall also the coming of the Son of man be." (Matt. 24:37; 2 Thess. 2:11; 2 Tim. 3:13; Jude 17–19, &c.)

4. *National and political revolutions and great disturbances.* "There shall be upon the earth distress of nations, with perplexity; the sea and waves thereof roaring; men's hearts failing them for fear, and for looking after those things which are coming on the earth; for the powers of heaven shall be shaken. And then shall they see the Son of man coming in a cloud, with power and

great glory." (Lu. 21:25–27; Heb. 12:27; Rev. 8:1–13; Is. 2:10–22, &c.)

5. *Numerous unusual physical phenomena, and portentous forebodings of nature.* "Great earthquakes shall be in divers places, and famines and pestilences; and fearful sights and great signs shall there be from heaven. And there shall be signs in the sun, and in the moon, and in the stars; and upon earth distress of nations. And then shall they see the Son of man coming in a cloud." (Lu. 21:11, 25, 27; Acts 2:19, 20; Micah, 7:15, 16.)

6. *An unusual awakening of interest and inquiry among the true followers of Christ respecting His second coming.* "At midnight there was a cry made. Behold the Bridegroom cometh; go ye out to meet Him." (Matt. 25:6; Hab. 2:1–3; Dan. 12:4, 9.)

7. *Unprecedented manifestations of the power and malice of the devil in the Church and in the world.* "The devil is come down unto you, having great wrath, because he knoweth that he hath but a short time." (Rev. 12:12; Matt. 24:24; 2 Thess. 2:8, 12; 1 Tim. 4:1, 3, &c.)

These and other signs are clearly indicated, and if we fail to look out for them, and to be influenced by them in our conclusions as to the approaching nearness of the grand event which they are designed immediately to anticipate, may we not meet with the displeasure of our Lord, and render ourselves obnoxious to the rebuke He administered to some of old; "O ye hypocrites, ye can discern the face of the sky; but can ye not discern the signs of the times?" (Matt. 16:3.)

But this opinion of the rapidly approaching period is not founded solely on "the signs" predicted; which leads us briefly to consider,

2. *The specific (chronological) time of the Second Advent.*

There are certain chronological predictions which have direct reference to this event; and which have not, surely, been given in order merely to awaken a curiosity never to be gratified, and to lead to vain and profitless speculation. If in ages past no satisfactory solution of these predicted times has been reached, *it is but the fulfilment of prophecy.* A celestial messenger said to Daniel (10:14), "I am come to make thee understand what shall *befall thy people in the latter days.*" In the twelfth chapter we read, "O Daniel, *shut up* the words and *seal the book even to the time of the end.*" And again: "Then said I; O my Lord! what shall be the end of these things? And he said, Go thy way, Daniel, for the words are closed up and sealed *till the time of the end.* . . . And none of the wicked shall understand, *but the wise shall understand.*" Thus are we informed that a time would come when, howsoever obscure and unintelligible to the wicked these predictions should be, "*the wise should understand them;*" for "at the time of the end" are these seals to be broken and the words understood. And we ask, who will say that the "time of the end" may not now have come? Within these thirty or forty years much attention has been given to the investigation of these "signs" of the times, and to the study of the chronological prophecies; and these investigations have been conducted by some of the most sober-minded, the most learned, and the most godly of the Church; and it is a very noteworthy fact that, with scarcely a single exception, the conclusion is reached, that within a few years, three, or five, or ten, these predicted events will transpire, or begin to be verified. All the lines of prophetic interpretation, the result of independent and of varied methods of investigation, seem most remarkably to converge to these very years now just at hand. It is thought, and with many it is a conviction, that within the period specified, the long anticipated second coming of the Son of man in the clouds of heaven, to glorify the saints, and to be glorified of them; to execute judgments upon His enemies; to establish His kingdom, and thus to inaugurate the Millennium, will occur, or, at least, that "the beginning of the end" will be most manifest. In reference to any specific, definite time when these events will transpire we wish to speak with caution. We have no opinion to express as the result of independent examination of the chronological prophecies. We refer to the conclusions which others have reached. A short time will test the correctness of these conclusions. They may prove fallacious. But those who entertain them think they have, after patient study, all-sufficient reasons for their belief. We do not give here the data on which their conclusions are founded, nor the varied investigations leading to them, but the simple result to which they have come; and this assuredly demands most serious consideration. For if it be legitimately reached, we are indeed standing on the very verge of that tremendous crisis, in which all the prophecies centre in regard to the interests and the destinies both of the Church of God and the nations of the earth, at the time of the great "harvest," at the end of the world, or the "times of the Gentiles."

We know that all attempts to fix definitely the time of these stupendous events is by many most strenuously opposed, and it is thought that there is decided scriptural warrant for the objection. Many of those who make it have no expectation of a literal kingdom with Christ, in person, the reigning Prince, *ever* being established here on earth. We have already noticed the intimation given to Daniel, that at "the time of the end" the seal of the book containing these mysteries should be broken, and the "wise should understand." We may now refer to some declarations of the Saviour, which to many are the assurance that the time is not to be known by any until the event shall be actually upon us.

Jesus said to the inquiry of the disciples, "Wilt thou *at this time* restore again the kingdom to Israel?" "*It is not for you to know the times or the seasons which the Father hath put in His own power.*" (Acts 1:6, 7.)

It is of some importance here to note, that so far from this response being a denial of His purpose to establish that kingdom which they expected would be here on earth, with Him as their Prince, it is a virtual admission that *it would be so established.* The Saviour would only remind them that it was not for *them* to know the *time* when it should be done. It is not for *you* to know—*you* of this generation, and it may have embraced many subsequent generations. It was in the *Father's power.* But if *they* were not to know the time, it does not follow that a knowledge of that time was always to be withheld from prayerful inquirers. It was in the Father's power not only to establish the kingdom, but to make known, if so He should be pleased to do, the time when it should be done; and especially as the period should arrive when, according to Daniel, "the wise would be made to understand" the contents of the sealed book; and when the "signs" of the times should clearly indicate the near approach of the great event. We see not that the response of the Saviour is to bar or to discourage inquiry on the subject.

A second passage which to some appears to be even more conclusive, as to the futility and impropriety of endeavoring to ascertain the time of the second advent, is the declaration of Jesus to His disciples as recorded, Mark 13:32; "Of that day and that hour knoweth no man; no, not the angels which are in heaven, neither the Son, but the Father." Not designing to make a special point of the fact that reference is here made not to the *year*, but to the *day* and *hour* of His coming, it is yet worthy of some note, inasmuch as the specific day and hour are not embraced in the calculation of any. But even if they were, we see not that this utterance of the Saviour forbids the hope of ascertaining them, much less does it prohibit positively or by implication, an endeavor by the study of chronological prophecy to discover what may be the *year*, proximately at least. Jesus declares that neither man nor angel, nor the Son of man "*knoweth*" the day and hour. And the truthfulness of the declaration no one may question. But who is the Son of man, and what is the date, and what were the circumstances of the utterance? The Son is the same One precisely, of whom it is said, He "*increased* in wisdom and stature and in favor with God and man." (Luke 2:52.) The same One who was, undoubtedly, in ignorance of some things, and it may be even of the time of His second coming, until the hour of His death. Christ was possessed of a twofold nature. He was perfect *man* as He was perfect God. How the human nature of Christ, in intimate union and sympathy with the divine, thus closely associated with Omniscience itself, could be limited in its knowledge, is not for us to explain. It is a mystery which we believe neither the writer nor the reader may comprehend. Still it is a fact, beyond question, that of some things, Christ, when in the flesh, was absolutely ignorant. Of the time of His predicted advent He was, when He spoke the words, as ignorant as was man or angel. But was He always to remain in ignorance of that time? Can He be ignorant of it as we write the sentence, or as the reader's eye may rest upon it? No one surely will affirm that now, as events are drawing to a crisis; now that the God-man is ordering His providences for the grand consummation, He knoweth not the time. "No man *knoweth.*" This was said eighteen hundred years since. This was then the state of knowledge on the subject. If the Son now knows the time, may not angels have learned it also? Has it not yet been revealed to those who are so intimately associated with that second coming? The Son of man is to come with "the holy angels." Are they yet to be apprised of this fact or of its nearness of approach, yea, of its definite period? While to these inquiries no absolutely positive answer may be given, it is, we affirm, a probability, approaching closely to a certainty, that it is a matter of absolute knowledge. And although "man" knew it not in the days of Christ's sojourn on earth, may he not learn it before the very time shall arrive, "lest that day come upon him unawares?" (Luke 21:34.) For an answer we refer again to the command to Daniel to seal up the prophecy "even to the time of the end," and the subsequent assurance that the seals should be broken and "the wise should understand;" (Dan. 12:4, 10;) and to the testimony of St. Paul, who declares that "the children of light are not in darkness that the day should overtake them as a thief." (1 Thess. 5:4, 5.) The great Reformer may not have been very presumptuous in His belief that, "God would yet raise up some one who should be able to reckon up the times, and with certainty hit upon the very day."[1]

Is there, we ask, anything in the word of God to forbid our hope and expectation that the Lord will, if He have not already done it, imbue some diligent students with "wisdom," so that at this "time of the end" they may "understand" the import of these predictions?

Nor may we be at a loss to discover why it was that the definite time was not made known to the immediate disciples of Christ, and why it was withheld from many subsequent generations. The wisdom and the goodness of God are manifest in this divine arrangement. "I find in this concealment," remarks Dr. Seiss,[2] "the great unsearchable wisdom of the Author of salvation, in so arranging what He has said about the time as to secure the *same practical effects* for every age, without confining the promise to any." And Bickersteth[3] remarks, in answer to the question, "Why did He withhold the time?" "Look back. You stand on the eminence of eighteen centuries. See what these centuries have been. Generation after generation, apostles, martyrs, fathers, confessors, and reformers, have lived and died. Mark all the conflicts through which the early Christians attained their triumphs, their labors, sufferings, persecutions, and martyrdoms. Go on to the rise of Popery and Mohammedanism; see the dark

[1] Luther; see Dr. Seiss's "Last Times," p. 260.

[2] "The Ten Virgins," p. 30. [3] "Time to Favor Zion."

ages; mark the struggles of infant Protestantism, and its subsequent decay. Look at the present spread of infidelity among professedly Christian nations. Had the Apostles been told, all this must previously take place—all this corruption must spread over the world—what needless despondency and heart-sinkings must have overwhelmed them! Eighteen hundred years of deferred expectation!—eighteen hundred years of Israel's dispersion and desolation!—eighteen hundred years yet to remain of the Gentile monarchies—and eighteen hundred years of the treading under foot of Jerusalem! With that wisdom and love which marks all the Lord's providence to His Church, this dark scene was kept back." Thus we see the wisdom and the goodness of the Saviour's answer to the questioning disciples; "It is not for *you* to know the times or the seasons which the Father hath put in His own power." He would have His people, in every age, reap the spiritual benefit of a cherished expectation of His coming. The animating, purifying, and heavenly hope of that event He would have them ever enjoy. Hence they were to watch for it; to anticipate it; to rejoice in it. There was to be a season of waiting. A knowledge of how long it was to be protracted He kindly withheld from them; that thus they might feel the power and influence of His oft-repeated injunction, "Watch; for ye know not when the Son of man cometh."

But it still may be asked, as it often has been;

"Wherefore dwell on these unfulfilled predictions? What profit are we to derive from the study of them?" Much every way, is the unhesitating reply of those who wait for and love Christ's appearing, as did the aged Paul when he anticipated the crown of righteousness, which he was to receive at the coming of his Lord.

We may now consider briefly—

III. The Practical Moral Bearing and Influence of the Doctrine of Christ's Second Coming.

If this doctrine of the personal coming of Christ before the Millennium be true; if this advent is (as we believe the Scriptures declare) to be preceded by, attended with, and followed by most stupendous events; if the Son of man is to come to raise from their graves the bodies of His saints, constituting "the first resurrection," "the resurrection of the just;" and if living believers, who shall be waiting for His coming, at the time, are to be caught up to meet Him in the air; if He is subsequently to appear in glory "with all His saints," visible to every eye, to take vengeance on His enemies, and to renovate this earth, purifying it by fire, and making it the fit abiding-place of His ransomed ones; if He will thus, at His coming, establish His kingdom in righteousness, and here personally with His risen saints judge or rule during the millennial period; and if we are to "watch" for this advent as for that which may occur at any time; then, surely, all will admit that the doctrine *should* have a direct salutary moral influence upon our lives and our feelings. It *should* operate most decidedly to make us more holy in conversation and more heavenly-minded. It should stimulate to the cultivation of every Christian grace. If with any who profess to embrace the doctrine, it does not bring forth these fruits of godliness, the reason must be looked for in other causes than the tendency of the belief. It is the testimony of those who *fully, without wavering or doubt,* receive this as the revelation of our Lord, that in their own experience there are realized powerful incentives to holy living—that they may be ready, with lamps trimmed and burning, and with oil in their vessels, to enter into the marriage feast, when the Bridegroom, for whose coming they are looking and praying, shall make His appearance. "For myself," remarks Ryle, "I can only give my own individual testimony; but the little I know, experimentally, of the doctrine of Christ's second coming, makes me regard it as most practical and precious, and makes me long to see it more generally received. I find it a powerful spring and stimulus to holy living; a motive for patience, for moderation, for spiritual-mindedness; a test for the improvement of time, and a gauge for all my actions."

This result is just what the whole tenor of the word of truth would lead us to expect. If attention has not been particularly drawn to the subject, it will, perhaps, be a matter of surprise to find that the prominent, we had almost said the exclusive motive to repentance, and to Christian diligence, and heavenly-mindedness and holiness of life, as urged in the Scriptures, is this very fact, the coming of the Lord Jesus Christ. If other considerations are presented, this stands pre-eminent as the one incentive and stimulus to duty. DEATH is that to which attention, in our day, is mainly directed as a motive to prepare for future retribution. It is, certainly, well calculated to arouse the attention of those who have but a brief probation here to spend. Death is the sealing of the destiny of the soul, as there is no further opportunity for repentance; and yet it is a fact well deserving serious reflection, that very seldom is any allusion made to death by the Saviour, in His discourses, or by the Apostles in their letters. We cannot recall a solitary instance where the sinner is exhorted to repentance, or the believer to diligence and holiness, in view of this event, so certain to all, so uncertain as to the time of its occurrence, and so momentous in its immediate and in its ever continuing consequences. It is not the motive urged home upon the conscience as a stimulus to effort. We do not mean to say that this may not be presented as a consideration well calculated of itself to make a deep impression. What we desire, particularly, to enforce, is, that it is not *the* scriptural motive—that which the Holy Spirit has presented as pre-eminently the most effective. In every epistle, except the brief ones, the Second and Third of John, and that to Philemon, there are allusions—and in several, very many allusions—to the second coming of Christ, as a motive to a holy life; whereas not one solitary reference, it is believed, is to be found to death as an incentive to the impenitent, or a stimulus to the believer. And, furthermore, it is worthy of note that the uniform testimony of the ministers of Christ is that there is scarcely a subject, if there be one, which is urged upon the attention of their hearers with so little *permanent* benefit as death. For upwards of thirty years has the writer preached the Gospel, and has sought for motives to urge the sinner to forsake his sins, and the Christian to increased devotedness; and many have been his appeals, at funerals and upon other occasions, based on the certainty of death, its solemnities and results, and he is constrained to declare that, so far as memory serves him, in but two solitary cases, and these doubtful ones, has he had evidence of any lasting benefit as the result of these appeals. Now why is it so? Death, wherever it occurs, makes a present solemn impression, awakens serious thought, and sometimes urges to resolutions of amendment. But where are to be found the *permanent* good results? They are confessedly but few. Do not men coolly discuss their plans of business and of pleasure even as they follow the corpse to the tomb? yea, often indulge in levity of feeling, and in the most trifling conversation? Why is it that these solemn admonitions, on the doings of death and in the very presence of the destroyer, so very generally fail to secure any abiding impressions for good? Why are our exhortations, and our warnings, in view of the opened grave, so barren of results? Can we find an all-sufficient, satisfactory answer in the thought, that the frequency of the occurrence so familiarizes the mind to the scene that susceptibility to salutary impressions is entirely or almost wholly lost? We think not. This may have, and undoubtedly has, its effect; but a solution of the question we must find in the fact that, agreeably to the Divine arrangement, as made known in the Scriptures, death is not the subject of appeal. Everywhere it is the second coming of our Lord.

But it may be inquired, as it has often been, is not death, to him who experiences it, to all intents and purposes, the same as the advent of Christ? And may we not understand by the expression, "The coming of the Son of man," where it is presented as a motive for watchfulness, this very providence? To both inquiries we are constrained to give an emphatic negative. Death and the coming of Christ are, in the Scriptures, widely contrasted. Death is the coming of the "king of terrors." It is in part the penalty of sin, a positive evil in itself, the result of Adam's apostasy. True, to the believer, it is, by the mercy of God, shorn of its terrors, and made a "gain;" only so, however, because of what sin hath brought upon our blighted earth. A "gain" only because we live in a world laboring under the curse; where life is a probation, a discipline;

and where no direct communion with Him who is the believer's hope and joy, and blessedness is had, except by faith. It is "gain" to depart and be "*with Christ.*" Death is, of itself, a positive evil, whereas the coming of the Son of man is represented as a glorious event. Nowhere is death presented as the object of watchfulness, and by no legitimate reasoning can we substitute the "coming of the Son of man" for it. At death, moreover, Christ does not *come* to the believer, but the believer goes to Him. He "*departs*" that he may be with Christ. At death "the dust [the body] shall return to the earth as it was; and the spirit shall return unto God who gave it." (Eccles. 12: 7.) Death is a present visitation, settling, it is true, the question of the soul's futurity. The advent of Christ is a predicted event; when the believer, as to his body, shall be raised from the grave, and a consummation of glory, not realized at death, will be his blessed experience; and when the sinner, knowing no joyous resurrection, will wait in "hades," or the intermediate state, with harrowing anticipations of the full infliction of his dread penalty at the closing act of the Judgment. (Rev. 20: 12.[1]) The exhortation to "watch for the coming of the Son of man," embraces much more than to watch for the approach of death. The mind is to be fixed on the stupendous, startling scenes which are connected with the second advent; and which are so intimately related, not only to the interests of indi-

[1] See p. 209.

viduals, but to those of the whole Church, and to the destinies of all nations. Read the comforting assurance of the Saviour to His sorrowing disciples. "In my Father's house are many mansions; if it were not so I would have told you. I go to prepare a place for you. And if I go and prepare a place for you"—what then? Is it "I will come to you at death that you may enjoy it?" Ah no; "I will *come again* and receive you unto Myself, that where I am there ye may be also;" referring them to His predicted second advent, as the time when this blessedness would be fully realized.

Nothing is more obvious than the marked prominence given in the New Testament to the practical moral bearing of the doctrine of the second advent.

Professor Hackett, of the Newton Theological Seminary, (who is not a millenarian,) a candid and distinguished commentator on the Acts of the Apostles, bears this testimony (p. 80); "The final coming of Christ was the great consummation on which the strongest desires of the souls of the first believers were fixed, and to which their thoughts and hopes were habitually turned. They lived with reference to this event. They labored to be prepared for it. They were constantly, in the expressive language of Peter, looking for and (in their impatience, as it were) hastening the arrival of the day of God. . . . . The Apostles, as well as the first Christians in general, comprehended the grandeur of that occasion. It filled their circle of view; stood forth, to their contemplation, as the point of culminating interest in their own and the world's history; threw into comparative insignificance the present time, death, all intermediate events, and made them feel that the manifestation of Christ with its consequences of indescribable moment to all true believers, was the grand object which they were to keep in view, as the end of their toils, the commencement and perfection of their glorious immortality. In such a state of intimate sympathy with an event, so familiar to their thoughts, they derived, and must have derived, *their chief incentives to action from the prospect of that future glory. As we should expect, they hold it up to the people of God to encourage them in affliction, to awaken them to fidelity, zeal, and perseverance;* and on the other hand, appeal to it to *warn the wicked and impress upon them the necessity of preparation for the revelations of that day.*" "If modern Christians," he continues to say, "sympathized more fully with the sacred writers on this subject, it would bring both their conduct and their style of religious instruction into nearer correspondence with the lives and teaching of the primitive examples of our faith."

This emphatic statement is fully confirmed by a reference to the Scriptures themselves. A few passages in illustration may be presented.

As an appeal to ministerial fidelity and diligence, hear St. Paul to Timothy; "I charge thee, therefore, before God and the Lord Jesus Christ, who shall judge the quick and the dead, *at His appearing and His Kingdom,* preach the Word; be instant in season, out of season; reprove, rebuke, exhort with all long-suffering and doctrine." (2 Tim. 4:1, 2.) So St. Peter; "'The elders which are among you I exhort, ... feed the flock of God, ... and when the *Chief Shepherd shall appear* ye shall receive a crown of glory that fadeth not away." (1 Pet. 5:2, 4.)

Are careless sinners to be aroused? "What is a man profited if he shall gain the whole world and lose his own soul; or what shall a man give in exchange for his soul? *For the Son of man shall come in the glory of His Father with His angels;* and then He shall reward every man according to his works." (Matt. 16:26, 27.) "Whosoever shall be ashamed of Me and My words, of him shall the Son of man be ashamed *when He shall come in His glory.*" (Luke 9:26.)

Are men called to repentance? "Repent ye, therefore, and be converted, that your sins may be blotted out, when the times of refreshing shall come from the presence of the Lord, *and He shall send Jesus Christ* . . . . whom the heavens must receive *until* the times of restitution of all things." (Acts 3:19, 21.)

Are saints exhorted to holiness of life and spirituality of mind? "When Christ who is our life *shall appear*, then shall ye also appear with Him in glory. Mortify, *therefore,* your members which are upon the earth." (Col. 3:4, 5.) "Denying ungodliness and worldly lusts, we should live soberly, righteously and godly in this present world; looking for that blessed hope, *and the glorious appearing of the great*

God and our Saviour Jesus Christ." (Tit. 2:12, 13.) "And now, little children, abide in Him; that, *when He shall appear*, we may have confidence, and not be ashamed before Him *at His coming.*" (1 John 2:28.)

Are patience, forbearance and long-suffering under persecutions and trials enjoined? "Seeing it is a righteous thing with God to recompense tribulation to them that trouble you; and to you who are troubled, rest with us; when the *Lord Jesus Christ shall be revealed* from heaven with His mighty angels, in flaming fire, taking vengeance on them that know not God, . . . when He shall come to be glorified in His saints." (2 Thess. 1:6–10.) "Be patient, therefore, *unto the coming of the Lord. . . .* Be ye also patient, stablish your hearts, for the *coming of the Lord draweth nigh.*" (James 5:7, 8.)

Is the advanced pilgrim to be cheered with the prospect before him? "I am now ready to be offered and the time of my departure is at hand. I have fought a good fight. I have finished my course. I have kept the faith. Henceforth there is laid up for me a crown of righteousness which the Lord the righteous Judge shall give me *at that day;* and not to me only but unto all them also that *love* His appearing." (2 Tim. 4:6, 8.)

Such are specimens of the many instances where the practical efficiency of this doctrine is presented. It stands forth in the Word of God, unequalled in its power to arouse the careless, to comfort the mourner, to incite to holiness of life, and to exalt the Saviour and His cross.

CHAPTER X.

A DIFFICULTY AND ITS ATTEMPTED SOLUTION —WATCHING CONSISTENT WITH UNFULFILLED PROPHECY.

WATCHING AN ENJOINED DUTY—COMING OF THE SON OF MAN IS NOT DEATH—HOW IS THE DUTY OF WATCHING CONSISTENT WITH UNFULFILLED PROPHECIES?—TWO CLASSES OF TEXTS REVEALING CHRIST'S SECOND ADVENT—TWO STAGES OF THE ADVENT—ONE A SECRET MANIFESTATION TO RAISE THE PIOUS DEAD—IT MAY BE SILENTLY DONE—THE LAST TRUMPET: WHAT IS IT?—THE DEAD CANNOT HEAR—AN INTERVAL BETWEEN THE STAGES OF THE ADVENT—A SOLUTION OF THE DIFFICULTY.

And what I say unto you I say unto all; Watch.—MARK 13:37.

THERE is nothing, perhaps, more frequently, and certainly nothing more emphatically, enjoined by the divine Teacher, than constant "watching" for His second coming. "Watch; for ye know not what hour your Lord doth come. . . . . Therefore be ye also ready; for in such an hour as ye think not the Son of man cometh." (Matt. 24: 42, 44.) "Watch; for ye know neither the day nor the hour wherein the Son of man cometh." (Matt. 25:13.) "Take ye heed, watch and pray;

for ye know not when the time is." (Mark 13:33.) "Watch ye and pray always, that ye may be accounted worthy to escape all these things that shall come to pass, and to stand before the Son of man." (Luke 21:36.) In perfect harmony with these solemn injunctions of the Saviour, are the frequent allusions to the subject by the inspired apostles. "Waiting for the coming of our Lord Jesus Christ." (1 Cor. 1:7.) "The Lord direct your hearts . . . . into the patient waiting for Christ." (2 Thess. 3:5.) "Looking for and hasting unto [or hastening] the coming of the day of God." (2 Pet. 3:12.) "Looking for that blessed hope, and the glorious appearing of the great God and our Saviour Jesus Christ." (Tit. 2:13.)

Now this "watching," this "waiting," this "looking for" the Son of man, whatever else it may embrace, does most assuredly imply expectation, anticipation of the event, as one which may be near at hand; one indeed which may occur at any moment. This no one will dispute. Nor can we admit that *figurative* interpretation of this "coming of the Bridegroom"—the "return of the Nobleman who had gone to receive a Kingdom," which would fritter down the grand, commanding fact of the literal coming of our Lord to the visitation of one's death. Nowhere can these expressions have this meaning; at least there is nothing connected with them which gives the slightest plausibility to the conjecture. And no one, we think, without an object to secure, or a special difficulty to escape, would ever conclude from the narratives connected with the injunctions, that such an explanation was tenable. No one, surely, can prove such to be their import. We consider it as wholly gratuitous.

The early disciples were commanded to watch, and so are we, with greatly increased and ever increasing emphasis, in these latter days. It is our duty *constantly* to watch—constantly to be waiting and looking for the personal coming of the Son of man. Now just here, is originated in some minds, a *difficulty*. We teach that certain grand events are to transpire before the full inauguration of the Millennium, or before the coming of Christ Jesus. Such as the full development and manifestation of "the man of sin," the antichrist; the literal restoration of the Jews to Palestine; a season of unparalleled tribulation, &c. And it is inquired, and we admit the inquiry to be perfectly natural and legitimate—how can we be "watching" and "waiting for," and thus constantly expecting, as an event which may at any time occur, that which, it is predicted will *not* take place until these other prophecies are fulfilled? That we may find a solution of the difficulty, let us now look at these passages which speak of the second coming of our Lord. And if we do not greatly err in judgment, we shall find two classes of texts, having a marked difference of allusion. Thus; "Watch, for ye know not what hour your Lord doth come. But know this—that if the good man of the house had known in what watch the *thief would come* he would have watched."

(Matt. 24:42; Luke 12:39.) "For yourselves know perfectly that the day of the Lord so cometh as a *thief in the night.*" (1 Thess. 5:2.) "The day of the Lord will come as a *thief in the night.*" (2 Pet. 3:10.) "Behold I come *as a thief.*" (Rev. 16:15.) Here is one class of texts. Now read again; "Hereafter shall ye *see* the Son of man .... *coming in the clouds of heaven.*" (Matt. 26:64.) "Ye men of Galilee, ... this same Jesus .... shall *so come in like manner* as ye have seen Him go into heaven." (Acts 1:11.) "Them also which sleep in Jesus will God *bring with Him.*" (1 Thess. 4:14.) "At the coming of our Lord *with all His saints.*" (1 Thess. 3:13.) "When the Lord Jesus shall be *revealed from heaven with His mighty angels,* in flaming fire, taking vengeance on them that know not God." (2 Thess. 1:7, 8.) "Behold He cometh *with clouds, and every eye shall see Him, and they also which pierced Him; and all kindreds of the earth shall wail because of Him.*" (Rev. 1:7.) Here is another class of predictions, all looking to the same grand event. Now does it not most plainly appear that there are to be two comings of the Lord, or rather, two separate, distinct stages, or manifestations of that coming? The one like "A THIEF" as it were; secretly, silently and invisible to the world at large. The other a visible manifestation of the Son of man in the clouds of heaven, when "*every eye shall see Him,*" and when He will be attended by "His saints?" But how will this be effected? When and how will He have gathered to Himself "His saints"—His

Bride—that they may come with Him? A solution of the question we have in the first class of passages. It will be at the first stage of His advent. This first stage may be a somewhat protracted period, during which the Lord may be secretly taking from their graves the slumbering dust of His saints, and then translating, it may be, some of His prepared and waiting ones; for we are told "one shall be taken and the other left;" the whole scene perhaps, closing with what may possibly be a more open exhibition of divine power and glory as described by the Apostle; "The Lord Himself shall descend from heaven, with a shout, with the voice of the archangel and with the trump of God, and the dead in Christ shall rise first. Then we which are alive and remain shall be caught up together with them in the clouds to meet the Lord in the air." (1 Thess. 4:16.) There are those who think that both the resurrection of the righteous, and the translation of the living, waiting ones, will be in part at least by gradual process, and silently carried on, and that this will meet all the statements of the Scriptures touching these deeply interesting facts. Dr. Seiss[1] remarks; "I suppose that the resurrection of the saints will conform to that of their Lord, and not occur visibly to men in the flesh. . . . So far as we know, nobody saw Christ rise. And it would seem as if the same stealth was to attend the translation of the saints. . . . . It was so that

[1] "Day of the Lord."

Enoch seems to have been stolen away from the earth." William Newton[1] remarks; "From the midst of the occupations of daily life they shall be taken. No sudden outburst of power—no circumstances of terror and of grandeur shall attend the taking. An invisible hand shall be stretched forth to take the living saint out of the midst of his unbelieving companions. In a moment it shall be done. In the twinkling of an eye."

"But," he adds, "it will be asked, is not the *sounding of the last trumpet* to be the signal for the rising of the dead? How then can we speak of it as silently going on?"

The Bible does speak of the *trump* of God. But we are not to suppose it to be a *material* trumpet, nor the sounding of it any more an audible noise than were the six previous trumpets of the Apocalypse, material instruments and their sounding attended by an audible noise. "These trumpets are *symbols*, and their sounding symbolized the occurrence of the events that were to take place under them. Six of the trumpets have already *sounded;* one yet remains—that is the *last.* It symbolizes a given event, that is *the going forth of Almighty Power* to arouse His sleeping dead." That this sounding is figurative, may, moreover, be inferred from the fact that it is to be *heard* by the *dead.* "The *dead* shall *hear* the voice," &c. The very fact of the *dead hearing* the sound, would seem clearly to intimate that it indicates the

[1] "Lectures on Daniel."

exercise of power to produce the effect rather than the literal arousing, by an audible sound, of what cannot in any sense be said to have the faculty of hearing. But it may still be urged, cannot *God* cause the dead bodies of His saints to hear? We answer no? And we do not feel that we are limiting the power of the Almighty in the slightest degree by this response. He cannot do an inconsistent or impossible thing. Can He, we inquire, cause the solid rocks literally to hear? Hearing is a faculty exclusively of an animated being. A dead stone cannot hear, nor can a dead human body. And all the passages where the dead are said to hear His voice, or where hearing is implied, mean nothing more than that, by the exercise of His power, the same effect is produced as would be did they actually hear, and hearing, obey His will. The sounding of the trumpet, therefore, is not, as many teach, the sending forth of an audible sound, but the exercise of a power to secure the result. Here the rising of the dead in Christ will be the proof that the archangel is fulfilling his commission. This last trump may be silently sounding for months and for years, as it was with the six preceding ones. It will sound until the last of His sleeping dead shall have arisen. This being done, we see how the Lord may be, subsequently, *openly revealed* for a very different purpose, which is to execute His judgment upon His enemies, bringing *His saints with Him*—that is His risen saints.

Here, then, we have these two distinct, separate

stages of the coming of the Son of man. Now we inquire who will venture to declare how long or how short an interval may intervene between these two manifestations? That there is an interval of some duration is obvious. But we are not aware that the length of it is anywhere revealed, nor do we know of any circumstance from which we may draw an inference that it is very brief. If any assert that one is immediately to succeed the other, we ask for the proof of it, and where the necessity? We know not wherein consists the one, nor where to find the other. For aught that the word of God declares, may there not be an interval of days, of months, of years; yea, an interval sufficiently long for the fulfilment of all the predictions which are to be verified before the Millennium? If no valid objection to this view of the subject be found, then have we a satisfactory solution of the difficulty in reference to the duty of watching. The first stage of the Lord's coming may be at any time—at any moment. He may, indeed, have already come? Who can assure me that no grave has been vacated of its occupant? Who can be sure that the Lord has not, as a *thief in the night*, already taken to Himself some of that precious dust over which He has watched for years or centuries? While we know not that He has, we dare not say that He has not.

Let us remember, that whether this or any other attempted solution of the difficulty be or be not satisfactory, one thing remains. It is our duty carefully to *watch* for the coming of the Son of man. The duty is ours, and any seeming difficulties that exist, we may rest assured, will be cleared up by Him whose word we are to obey, and who hath in His own hands the ordering of all these events. We may possibly not know how to meet fully all the objections of the skeptic in reference to the great events immediately before us; but there is One who does know how to confound the "wisdom of the wise," and to put to shame the scoffing taunts of those who impiously inquire, "Where is the promise of His coming?" And in the mean time let us "receive with meekness the engrafted word, which is able to save our souls," (James 1:21,) and be found with our loins girt about and our lamps trimmed, waiting for the coming of the BRIDEGROOM.

It has been well remarked,[1] in reference to the revelations of the Scriptures touching this one grand, central truth, the coming of the Son of man: "All the holy prophets, since the world began, have borne their testimony to this great truth. Indeed, the first and second coming of Christ stand out as mountain peaks on the plain of God's word. They catch the first and last rays of His light. The earliest beams of His truth play upon them; and the latest rays from heaven linger and glow on their summits. Long before the plain between them receives the light; long before the truths which are intermediate to them

[1] W. Newton on Daniel.

are revealed, they are made known. The living sunlight of revelation brings them distinctly out, while yet other truths, and great, practical, and glorious truths too, are in the dark. The prophecies, in reference to the first, have long since been fulfilled. And now all the predictions turn to the second as the one living hope of the Church. Preparation for it is our instant duty. It gives power and point to every appeal. It underlies every hope. It urges to and quickens in every duty. It is the consummation of the first; the harvest of the world; all before it is but a preparation.

"Well, brethren," he inquires, "what is all this to you? This coming of the Lord of glory? What is your relation to it? This is just the one question infinitely more momentous than any other. Gather together all the interests of earth; place them in the light of this truth: and how utterly worthless they appear. Its riches, and honors, and pleasures; what are all these? Will they avail you at that hour? Will the honors of the great man, and the wealth of the rich man, and the wisdom of the wise man, profit him then? He may have wielded earth's mightiest sceptre. Armies may have moved at his command; or senates thrilled with his eloquence; or nations trembled at his power. But what will all this avail? The wisdom of this world gives no answer to the question, 'Who shall stand when He appeareth?' "

And, surely, He will appear. The roll of

Heaven's grand purposes is unfolding fast. Men may close their eyes to the impending scenes, and their ears to the prophetic intimations; but the Lord is carrying on His grand, His mighty preparations, with a steady hand and a determined will; and foolish, slumbering virgins in the Church, and scoffing skeptics without; both of whom may have laughed to scorn the truth, with the inquiry, "Where is the promise of His coming?" will be startled from their fancied security, as the cry shall go forth with an emphasis no one may disregard; not, it may be, "Behold, the Bridegroom *cometh!*" but, "Behold, the Bridegroom has *already come!*" for the signs of the times which betokened His coming they shall have wilfully disregarded.

"*What I say unto you, I say unto all*, WATCH; for ye know not when the hour cometh. Watch, therefore. Blessed is that servant whom the Lord, when He cometh, shall find so doing."

CHAPTER XI.

SUMMARY AND CONCLUSION.

SUMMARY OF MILLENARIAN DOCTRINES — THE SUBJECT DEMANDS CONSIDERATION — IMPROPRIETY OF REJECTING IT WITHOUT INVESTIGATION — SOME INEXPLICABLE DIFFICULTIES — MILLENARIANISM CLEARS UP MANY OBSCURE PASSAGES—THE DUTY OF WATCHING.

Now of the things which we have spoken this is the sum.
HEB. 8:1.

IT has been our purpose, in the preceding pages, to present the prominent teachings of Millenarianism, with a portion of the scriptural evidence by which the views are believed to be established. It may not be unprofitable, before we close the discussion, to pass in brief review these several topics, in their connection, and to consider a few themes naturally suggested by them, and which are worthy of most serious reflection.

We have traced the Jewish people from their origin, onward through successive generations; showing the exact fulfilment of prophecy, in the repeated changes they have experienced, up to their present wide-spread distribution amid the nations of the earth. We have noted the wonderful phenomenon, perfectly unique in its nature, of their retaining their distinct nationality, notwithstanding their wide dispersion, and the multiplied influences designed and well calculated to merge them in the various nations among whom they have been scattered. Living, often, intimately among them, and yet, in their social and religious views and habits, most widely separated. The peculiarities of their condition find no possible solution, but in a special divine providence which has most signally watched over, guided, and preserved them, for the accomplishment of a divine purpose. That purpose is their regathering from amid the nations, and their literal restoration to the land of Palestine—a land secured to them by positive covenant engagement. Their fondly cherished hopes are to be realized, and the truthfulness of Jehovah vindicated by their return to the abode of their fathers. This inheritance of which they are to become possessed, has been as signally preserved for them as they have been preserved for it. "Jerusalem has long been 'trodden down' of the Gentiles; but no one set of Gentiles has been allowed to tread it for any length of time. It has been successively occupied by the Romans, the Persians, the Saracens, the Turks of the Seleucian race, the Egyptian Caliphs, the Latin Christians, the Egyptian Caliphs a second time, the Mamelukes, and the Turks of the Ottoman race. And by this ceaseless change of occupants, it has been very plainly hinted that all were intruders and usurpers, and that the rightful owner had not yet appeared. . . . . Christians and Infidels, Papists and Mohammedans, Franks and Saracens, Turks and Egyptians, have all fought for the Holy City, and possessed it by turns; but never have any of them been able to keep it long. And whilst, in their struggles for its custody, the Gentiles have trodden Jerusalem down, the persecuted people, whose it is, await in calm assurance the day when the Lord himself shall put them in perpetual possession."[1]

This restoration is to be preceded by a national repentance; and to be followed by a recognition and acknowledgment of the crowning sin of their ancestors, and one which they themselves, by their course, have fully sanctioned and indorsed, —the rejection of their Messiah eighteen centuries since. Established in Palestine, with Jerusalem their metropolis, they are again to enjoy, and in a degree never previously experienced, the benediction of the Lord. Their recognized Messiah is to be their Prince and Sovereign; and He is graciously to rule not only over them, but the dominion of the whole earth is to be given unto Him. Thus, as immediately connected with the restoration of the Hebrew people, will be the predicted and long-anticipated second coming of our Lord to establish His Kingdom, over which He will literally and in person reign, the incarnate God-man, Christ Jesus. He will occupy the throne of David, fulfilling thus the predictions

[1] Rev. James Hamilton.

of holy prophets, and re-establishing the Theocracy here on earth.

This restoration of the Jews will be amid startling national revolutions, and Christ will come as the Lord supreme to execute righteous judgment upon His persistent enemies, and to manifest signal favor to His people, the subjects of His elective love. This will be seen in the overthrow of all that shall be found to oppose His authority; the destruction of the wicked nations and the adherents of all antichristian systems; and in the resurrection of the bodies of His sleeping saints —"the first resurrection"—and the translation with them of all the then living, who shall have joyfully waited for His coming, to His pavilion in the clouds, until the fiery visitation of the Lord's displeasure upon the wicked shall have passed away. This earth, thus regenerated, purified, and freed from its bondage, shall be the fit abiding-place of the honored subjects of His kingdom. These will be the days of millennial glory, during which Satan is to be bound, and excluded from the earth, where, during this dispensation, he shall have exercised his unrighteously usurped authority as the permitted god of this world (aion)—this age or dispensation.

These thousand years, or the Millennium, will be a period of universal righteousness and peace. It will be the promised kingdom of our Lord. The saints of "the first resurrection," and those translated at the coming of Christ, will be participants with Him in the administration of the kingdom, exercising an authority and occupying a position which we may not now fully comprehend, but which will be of peculiar honor. The subjects of the government will be those who, living at the time of the "appearing" of Christ, shall escape the judgments inflicted upon the conspicuously wicked, and their descendants. These, we believe, will continue to increase, not only during the millennial reign, but for successive generations forever. They will be the blissful occupants of the new, the purified, regenerated earth, and will constitute that wondrous host of the redeemed, which, as to number, like the "stars of heaven," "the sands of the sea," and "the dust of the earth," no man may calculate.

Thus the second, personal, visible coming of the Saviour in glory and with His saints is to precede the Millennium; which is, indeed, to be ushered in, and not followed by it. For this joyously and long anticipated period is not to be introduced by the gradual extension of Gospel truth, accomplished by instrumentalities now employed by the Church, until all nations shall be brought into subjection to the will of God. The moral condition of the race is to remain much as it now is. The evil will continue to preponderate over the good, or, at least, to be intimately intermixed. The tares will continue to be intermingled with the wheat until the great harvest. Then the separation shall be made; and the harvest will be at the personal coming of our Lord, and not before. It will be at the "end of the world,"—

the end of the age. In the meantime a great, a glorious work is to be accomplished by the vigorous, untiring missionary efforts of the people of God, which is to gather from all nations unto Christ the elect of Heaven's grace. To these nations the Gospel of the kingdom is to be preached "for a witness." And then shall the end come. This period—or that during which the second advent of the Son of man is delayed—is the time and the fulness of the Gentiles. Whilst it continues Jerusalem is to be trodden down, the land remain a waste, and the Jewish people scattered and persecuted. The kingdom of righteousness being established, with Christ upon the throne of David, and Satan a prisoner in the fearful abyss, the predicted thousand years of millennial righteousness will be enjoyed. This being ended, and Satan loosed for a season, he will make his last desperate effort to destroy the Holy City and the people of God; which will result in his discomfiture and overthrow, to be followed by the closing act of the Judgment day. This Judgment day will commence with the Saviour's coming before the Millennium, the first grand act of which will be the punishment of the living antichristian nations; the overthrow of the mystery of iniquity; the destruction of the fully developed "man of sin," the predicted antichrist; and "the first resurrection," and the translation of the saints. It will continue, as the rule or government of Christ during the Millennium, to close with the overthrow of the confederated hosts of Jehovah's enemies, the appearance of the Judge upon the great white throne, the resurrection of the wicked of all past generations, and their being cast into the dreadful "lake," the fitting abode of the unholy, and the fitting recompense of iniquity.

This restoration of the Jewish people, this second, personal, visible coming of the Son of man, this resurrection of the pious dead, this destruction of the wicked, and this commencement of the millennial kingdom, are, we have reason to believe, near at hand. They are to be preceded by specific signs, which are to indicate the proximate nearness of the period. These signs appear to be in the process of development, and hence we infer, the time of the glorious Epiphany cannot be far removed. The chronological prophecies, moreover, as interpreted by candid, diligent, prayerful, sober-minded Christian students, point to a period embraced within the coming few years, when all that the Church has hoped and longed for, all that holy seers of the former dispensation loved to portray, and all that the inspired Apostles and the Redeemer Himself anticipated of the "glory that should follow," shall begin to be accomplished in the revelation from heaven of Him who is to reign in righteousness.

Such are a part of the series of startling but glorious events which, we believe, are literally to transpire; and to commence, it may be, within a short period; a period, certainly, we have reason to conclude, embraced by the lifetime of many, yea, of most who are now living upon earth, heedless of the voice which admonishes all to be ready for the coming of the Bridegroom.

In view of this subject we remark:

FIRST. That if there be but the semblance of proof from the word of God that these things are so—nay, even if there be but the thought of a mere possibility that they may be true, it surely becomes every one who anticipates coming retribution carefully to investigate the subject, inasmuch as momentous consequences are involved in a right understanding of the declarations of Jehovah touching these great themes. But what should be the interest awakened, when, as we unhesitatingly maintain, there is not merely the semblance of proof—not a possibility that these things are revealed, but an array of evidence, such that but very few are found to give the subject prayerful and adequate attention, without a deep conviction of its truthfulness. Surely it calls for investigation; so that if it be rejected, it may be done intelligently, and warranted by satisfactory proof of its being a delusion, the suggestion of fanatical minds. Or, if found to be in very deed the word of God, it may be embraced, and the Master thus honored in the joyous looking for of His appearance. Many, we know, by examining the prophetic Scriptures, have adopted these views. Many more, and the number is daily increasing, are now willing to search the Scriptures to see if these things be so; and are yielding up their prejudices and long cherished opinions, before the force of convincing evidence. We thank God for these indications of good. But, while we thus rejoice, our joy is intermingled with much pain, to know that there are those who are unwilling to give the subject any attention; satisfied apparently with the conviction, that what their fathers believed, and what they have been taught from their childhood to be the truth, must in very deed be the revelation of the Word. Some spurn the whole subject as one of idle speculation, unprofitable, injurious, indeed, to the interests of the Saviour's kingdom, and hence to be repudiated and condemned.

We have no fault to find with any, who, after a careful, prayerful, thorough investigation, reach this conclusion; although we see not how they reach, or upon what basis they found their conclusion. Still they are to be honored for their candid examination, and for their intelligent condemnation. But to denounce the doctrines without investigation—to cry out "heresy," without knowing, or caring to know, what the heresy, without caricature, is, and by what proof it is attempted to be established, is evincive of a prejudice, and a perversion of sound principle which must fall under the ban of severest censure. It should ever be remembered that we are not to permit prejudice, and preconceived opinions, and long cherished theories, to take the place of scriptural argument. A subject of this kind, which, we maintain, is to be established by the Scriptures, is to be refuted—if so it may be—only by an appeal to the same sure word. No argument is worthy the theme—no argument can be legitimately used in its refutation, aside from the explicit teachings of the oracles of truth. And we must be permitted to insist that those who declare the pre-millennial advent of the Redeemer, and its associated truths, to be "a strong delusion," to which "God has given over some to believe a lie," should establish their position by a direct appeal to the same great fountain of wisdom to which we profess to appeal for the truthfulness of the one we occupy. Nothing short of this can satisfy those to whom these doctrines have become so precious. To arguments legitimately drawn from the oracles of God, all, we may venture to say, who think with us, hold themselves in readiness to give heed. And with grateful hearts will they thank those who may, in this way, reclaim them from their errors, if, indeed, they be under a delusion. We profess to seek, and to earnestly desire to know the truth. We think, in reference to these great themes, we have found it. It has cost us time. It has cost us painful mental struggles with prejudices deeply rooted, with early impressions, and with conclusions reached by a partial, one-sided investigation. But the conviction *has* been reached; and until evidence from the Scriptures be adduced against that conviction, as strong at least as that we find in its favor, we cannot yield it, although a host continue to oppose and brand it as fanaticism.

We ask that the Bible be read and understood as we read and understand any other book. That there are mysteries which no one may comprehend; difficulties which no human, if any finite mind, may fully solve, is freely admitted. And true is it that there are some particulars touching these views we have presented, which we may not explain, and that because the explanation is not definitely revealed; and some questions which an inquiring mind and an awakened curiosity may desire to have answered, to which we can give no adequate or positive response, simply because the Lord has left them unanswered in His word. But the prominent truths, those we need to know, are clearly stated. And we see not why, in order to understand them, we should resort to measures adopted in the study of no other book. Why should we, in one part of the Scriptures, resort to a strictly literal interpretation, and in another, where the statements are as plainly and clearly made, give to it all a figurative or spiritual import? To this question a satisfactory answer must be given before we admit its validity.

With prayerful, candid minds should we then address ourselves to this study; willing and determined to believe that the Revelator meant just what His words imply. So that when He assures us that a specific event shall occur in the future. we may anticipate its literal fulfilment. If He assured the early disciples that the Holy Ghost should be imparted unto them, they were to look for a literal verification of His words. They *were* thus verified on the day of Pentecost. If He as clearly and as plainly assures us that He will come again in glory to establish His kingdom, and to rule in righteousness on earth, are we not as fully to believe that He will thus come, and for this very purpose? If His first advent was anticipated by holy men of old as a literal, personal advent—they understanding the prophetic intimations as not admitting a mere figurative, allegorical, or spiritual fulfilment—so must we believe that the prophecies which predict His second coming, in language as distinct, and plain, and definite, claim from us a conviction of their accomplishment in His literal, personal, pre-millennial, second advent. The former predictions were literally verified; so will be the latter.

SECONDLY. Many portions of the word of God, otherwise more or less obscure, are freed of all difficulty when viewed in the light of these doctrines. We have often been delightfully surprised at thus discovering the import of passages of which we had sought, but in vain, a satisfactory explanation.

Thus we see how the saints—the people of God—are to *inherit* and *possess* the *earth*. Thus we understand more fully, and much more to our satisfaction, many of the parables, as that of the Tares and the Wheat; that of the Net, gathering up both good and bad; that of the Sower, asserting the very partial reception of the truth throughout this dispensation; that of the Leaven, giving to the word a meaning which it has in every other passage where it occurs; making it a principle of evil and not of good. Thus, again, the second Psalm has a richness of significancy and a specialty of reference, which every interpretation, aside from these views, fails to reach. Thus we understand the frequent allusions to the resurrection, and their particular reference, such as, "that they might obtain a *better* resurrection." (Heb. 11:35.) "Thou shalt be recompensed at the resurrection of *the just*." (Luke 14:14.) "If by any means I might attain unto the resurrection of [or from among] the dead." (Phil. 3:11.) "They are the children of God, *being* the children of *the* resurrection." (Luke 20:36.) "The *first* resurrection." (Rev. 20:5.) The former of these, and similar expressions, find their special significancy in the last, "the *first* resurrection:" clearly indicating something more and other than a promiscuous, simultaneous uprising of the righteous and the wicked. Thus, moreover, the condition of the moral state of society at the coming of the Saviour, comparing it with that in the days of Noah and of Lot, is perfectly clear to our understanding when applied to the condition of things at the close of the present dispensation, when the Son of man shall literally come. (Matt. 24:37–41; Luke 17:26–37.) Again, Rom. 8:19–23, has to the Millenarian no obscurity. The creature—the creation—"Ktisis," this sin-cursed earth, is to be freed from its bondage of corruption when those who, "groaning within themselves, and waiting for the adoption," shall experience "*the redemption of the body.*" Again we find a satisfactory solution of the difficulty presented by 1 Cor. 6:2; Matt. 19:28; Luke 22:29, 30; Rev. 20:4, and similar passages. "The saints shall judge the world." "They lived and reigned with Christ." "Ye who have followed me, in the regeneration when the Son of man shall sit on the throne of His glory, *ye also* shall sit upon twelve thrones, judging the twelve tribes of Israel." "I appoint unto you a kingdom, as my Father hath appointed unto me; that ye may . . . sit on thrones, judging the twelve tribes of Israel." It is not, the saints *do now* judge the world, but they *shall* judge it. It is not that the Apostles do *now* sit on thrones; but they *shall* do so; referring most clearly to a period beyond this life; beyond, indeed, this present dispensation. We may not precisely define, nor may we now be able fully to comprehend what is meant by this judgeship or rule of the saints and of the Apostles. They are, we know, to exercise the office under and in conjunction with Christ. It is to be a participation with Him, in some degree, of His authority and government, a position typified, it may be, by that of the judges of Israel of old. Again, the graphic description by Isaiah of old, of a conquering Prince coming up from Bozrah, with garments sprinkled with the blood of vanquished enemies (63:1–6), has a richness of import which can alone be apprehended and appreciated by viewing it as a prediction of the victories which are to be gained by the Saviour over His enemies at His second personal advent.

These views, again, clear up a difficulty, which, we presume, many have found in their attempts to interpret the scene described by St. Matthew (25 : 31–46),—a scene so generally referred to what is supposed to be the winding up of all terrestrial things subsequent to the Millennium—at the "day of Judgment." The difficulty of which we speak lies in the *ground* of approval and of condemnation of the several parties. We are elsewhere assured that, in the judgment of individuals, special attention is to be given to the secrets of the heart. External actions are to be judged of in the light of feeling, purpose, motive. Hidden things are to be brought to light. The counsels of the heart are to be made manifest. And the sentence of the Judge will have direct regard to these, the outward acts being but the reflection of what exists within. Here, however, there is no allusion whatever to these motives, and to this condition of the inner man. The grounds of judgment are, exclusively, the performance, or the neglect of outward deeds in reference to the needy, suffering children of God. Now, on the principle that this is meant to be descriptive of what is termed the General Judgment, limited to the closing scene of earth's eventful drama, when all will be judged and recompensed according to the individual character, how are we to account for the fact, that the ground of condemnation and acquittal is exclusively external deportment? Is this in accordance with the plainly revealed criterion of God's judgment of individual desert? But all difficulty is at once removed when we consider this judgment scene to be one of "nations," as the text declares it to be, and not of individuals—living nations, nations actually existing at the time, and that time the second coming of Christ to introduce the Millennium. Such a judgment must necessarily, in its decisions and awards, be based on external deeds of good and evil.

Again, we now may see the propriety, and comprehend the definite bearing of the Saviour's repeated command to *watch* for His coming. If that coming or manifestation in glory is not to be until *after* the Millennium, the word "watch" must have been used with a special and important modification of its meaning. To "watch for," most obviously implies *expectation*, and *uncertainty* also as to the precise time when the event or the person should transpire or appear. Now, if a thousand years of millennial blessedness are certainly to intervene between the time when the Saviour gave the injunction and the actual coming of the Son of man, must not the disciples have failed to see the propriety and force of it, if the word was to be understood in its ordinary acceptation? How are *we* to understand it, if the "coming of the Son of man" may not be near at hand, and to certainly occur before the predicted thousand years shall commence? We confess the experience of a serious difficulty in former efforts to comprehend the meaning of the Saviour's injunction: a difficulty which exists no longer. We are not much surprised, in view of this cause of embarrassment, that with those who are unwilling to suppose that the Divine speaker meant anything less than what the word "watch" suggests to every mind, there should be the supposition that by "the coming of the Son of man" is meant the coming or visitation of death! An interpretation which, we maintain, has no countenance whatever in the Scriptures; but one to which we appear to be absolutely driven, if we reject the pre-millennial, personal coming of our glorious Prince. These are a few of the passages the exposition of which is freed from the difficulty and obscurity of any other explanation. We present them as specimens.

There remains another subject of marked interest, upon which much light is cast by the views we advocate, and which is our last topic under this remark. It is the assured result of the glorious work of human redemption. We have often wondered at—we have, indeed, not unfrequently been greatly perplexed when considering the plan by which so large a portion of our race would be lost. For, with the views we entertained, we found it difficult to reach the conclusion, that if the lost of Adam's posterity were not actually to be a majority, they would fall but little below it. We could not well understand how "the wondrous plan" should accomplish comparatively so little in reference to the myriads of earth's inhabitants. The people of God are now, ever have been, and, up to the close of the present dispensation, will, we believe, continue to be, "a little flock." The vast, the immensely vast majority must be among the eternally miserable. We have reckoned in the redeemed of the millennial season, and the hopefully saved of the infant dead, and have thus found partial relief. It was, however, but partial. For making the aggregate as large as facts would warrant, the embarrassing question would be still suggested, why so large a number—a number, apparently, almost reaching, if it did not actually reach, that of the saved—must be lost! Why does the work of the devil, in its results, compare so painfully with that of the astounding work of the incarnate Jehovah? No one, it is true, may state the precise relative proportion of the lost through Satan and the saved through Christ, as enumerated by those who reject our views. But we again and emphatically ask, if the minds of many such do not often painfully labor at any attempt to settle the question? Not because the definite number may not be ascertained; but because of the conclusion to which the calculation seems fearfully to tend. Can they by any process of calculation and comparison reach a solution such as satisfies the Christian heart in reference to the result of Satanic malice and of the redemptive scheme? Do not those who believe that the personal coming of the Son of man in Judgment is to be at the end of the Millennium, and that that coming is to close up forever the history of our earth in its annihilation by a fearful conflagration, often experience an embarrassment, of which they would most gladly be relieved; and of which they cannot be, but by referring it all to the wisdom of Him who rules on high? But while all these matters must be referred to Him, we still may find, we are persuaded, relief to our burdened spirits, and great satisfaction in the assurances of the Bible, as we understand them. The work of Christ's redemption, in its results touching the number of the saved, is not to close, it is affirmed, with the thousand years of millennial blessedness. This earth is not to be renewed and fitted up for the occupants of the race of Adam merely during that joyous period. It is to be for the perpetual inheritance of the saints. And the work of salvation is to go on for an indefinite period, and, as many believe, and as the Scriptures seem to intimate, through successive generations forever. Thus all who are to inherit the earth at the coming of the Son of man; or all with so few exceptions, that, we may say, all who shall occupy it during the Millennium; and certainly all who shall, in even increasing numbers, occupy it afterwards, when "the new heavens and the new earth" of St. John (Rev. 21:1) shall be revealed, will be saved by the precious blood of Christ. Now does His atoning sacrifice—the glorious work of the incarnate Son of God in the absolutely inestimable greatness of its results—loom up before the mind, casting in the shade the result of Satanic malice, and causing the comparative number of its wretched victims to dwindle down to the merest fraction. It is as finite to infinitude. Truly, the number of the subjects of the grace of God shall be, as St. John in prophetic vision realized, "a great multitude, which no man could number." (Rev. 7:9.) The number of the finally lost will admit of computation, while that of the redeemed will defy the estimate of human or angelic minds. No such comparisons as those used to show the indefinite, the absolutely incalculable number of the redeemed, are anywhere used when speaking of the lost. No finite creature can possibly grasp a number without limit! Is not the Saviour thus gloriously exalted? Are not the results of the work of salvation to be somewhat commensurate with the incomprehensible greatness and glory of a God incarnate seeking the redemption of a lost world? Satan shall have no occasion to glory in his work of madness. The painfully embarrassed and laboring mind of the inquirer here finds rest, as, in anticipation of the issue of a Saviour's advent to our world, He, in sympathy with the angelic and holy host, exclaims, "Blessing, and honor, and glory, and power, be unto Him that sitteth upon the throne, and unto the Lamb forever and ever." (Rev. 5:13.)

THIRD. The propriety and duty of "watching" for the Son of man are obvious, and are based on a twofold consideration. The Saviour has positively and repeatedly enjoined it, and no one may fail to do it without dereliction of duty to Him whose word is law to all His faithful followers. But, moreover, the very nature of these anticipated events, and their relation to us personally, suggest and enforce the propriety of earnest, constant watching. The signs of the times indicate their near approach. It may be at any moment. Hence we should watch; and more especially because our dearest interests are connected with the exercise. If the events be of the significant character of which we speak; if they will be most grand, and startling, and sublime; and if the consequences of their advent will be so intimately associated with, not only the destinies of the nations of the earth, but with the eternal destiny, the everlasting weal or woe of individual souls, then is the exercise of continuous watching not only a duty, but a blessed privilege. The benediction of the Saviour Himself rests upon those whom He shall find "so doing" at His coming.

That all who read these pages may be thus "blessed," is the earnest prayer of one who desires to keep himself in readiness for the glorious appearing of the Son of man, and who puts forth this humble effort with the hope that he may induce others to seek and secure the appropriate readiness, ere it be too late, by a prayerful examination of the subject, and a yielding of the heart to the influence of the truth.

INDEX OF SUBJECTS.

INDEX OF TEXTS.

Jeremiah.

Ezekiel.

Daniel.

Hosea.

Joel.

Amos.

Micah.

Habakkuk.

Zechariah.

Matthew.

Mark.

Luke.

www.ingramcontent.com/pod-product-compliance
Lightning Source LLC
LaVergne TN
LVHW010224110826
845151LV00004B/1179

9781425526450